LANGUAGE SYSTEMS
AFTER PRAGUE STRUCTURALISM

edited by
LOUIS ARMAND
with
PAVEL ČERNOVSKÝ

Litteraria Pragensia
Prague 2007

Published 2007 by Litteraria Pragensia
an imprint of Charles University, Prague
Filozoficka fakulta, Náměstí Jana Palacha 2
116 38 Praha 1, Czech Republic

This volume is an outcome of the European Thematic Network Project ACUME2: "Interfacing Science, Literature and the Humanities," sub-project 1, University of Bologna.

This volume has been published with the support of the Socrates Erasmus programme for Thematic Network Projects through grant 227942-CP-1-2006-1-IT-ERASMUS-TN2006-2371/001-001 SO2-23RETH, funded with support from the European Commission. This publication reflects the views only of the authors and the Commission cannot be held responsible for any use which might be made of the information contained therein.

Cataloguing in Publication Data

Language Systems. After Prague Structuralism, edited by Louis Armand with Pavel Černovský. — 1st ed.
        p.   cm.
        ISBN 978-80-7308-171-3 (pb)
        1. Critical Theory.   2. Philosophy of Language.   3. Semiotics.
        I. Armand, Louis. II. Černovský, Pavel. III. Title

Printed in the Czech Republic by PB Tisk
Design by lazarus

Contents

Introduction
Language Systems,
or the Progress of Aporias

Three "tentatives" in lieu of an introduction ...

1. Frontiers of Theory

Theories of structure have always had to contend with an observer paradox, that in subjecting any structure or system to "observation," even to say in theorising it, theory either impinges upon its reality or affects it, and that thereby theories of structure are first and foremost invested in a dynamic that prohibits any straightforward delineation of its object let alone a "mediation" of its object within a closed system of knowledge. Whereas this aporia of theoretical limits and immersive environments in the past often gave rise to various dichotomies of subjectivism and objectivism, a body of experimental thought coming increasingly to the fore in the course of the twentieth century has proposed what is both a "discursive" and "recursive" thinking of aporias—of unresolvable structures of paradox or contradiction—and hence of the limits of theory and of what are sometimes referred to as "language systems."

Perhaps the most dramatic provocation to this mode of thinking is that which has arisen from the work of Werner Heisenberg and Niels Bohr, who in 1925 resolved the early paradoxes of "quantum physics" with a radical re-interpretation of dynamics. As Hans-Peter Dürr has written, this interpretation "demanded a revolution in what had been the classical view of the world, with the surprising recognition that matter is not really material at all, but a web of relationships, a kind of gestalt, or in a certain way 'information' without any carrier."[1]

---

[1] Hans-Peter Dürr, Daniel Dahm and Rudolf Prinz zur Lippe, *Potsdamer Denkschrift* (München: oekom verlag München, 2005) 3.

The consequence of approaching dynamics in non-objective, or relational, terms has born a certain amount of strange fruit over the decades, ranging across often disparate fields of enquiry, from psychiatry to game play, from semiotics and linguistics to human resource management, artificial intelligence and the World Wide Web. Notions of interactivity have come to proliferate in a world of increasingly mobile tele-information systems and surveillance-based knowledge and control systems, genetic modification and predictive modelling. The term "interactivity" itself is fraught with potential contradictions and paradoxes, nevertheless the implications of recursivity, feedback, and immersion upon a genealogy of thought that brings into constellation a general category of "theories of structure"—from quantum mechanics to deconstruction and cyber-theory—have transformed the ways in which we posit the limits of knowledge and undertake the work of theorising.

Today, there are at least six areas in which the popular imagination intersects with ideas emanating from contemporary theories of structure:

+ Ecologies and climate systems
+ Economics and social-demographics
+ Biogenetics and nanotechnology
+ Cosmological modelling and particle physics
+ Cybernetics and cyberculture
+ The military-industrial-entertainment complex

These areas, as we know, are heavily intersected by discourses from the social and human sciences, the arts, and popular culture. Each has extended our thinking about structure, whether in terms of dynamics, systematicity or discursivity, and in doing so have reconfigured the way we pose problems concerning such things as consciousness, reality and representation. For this reason, we can also look to the work of Peirce, Freud and Saussure for antecedents to a line of thinking that arrives at recent and contemporary discussions of new media, technicity and the "posthuman condition"—in the work, for example, of Bateson, McLuhan, Baudrillard, Deleuze and De Landa.

Above all, contemporary theories of structure demand that we confront the question not only of our technological circumstances, nor simply the technologically inflected character of our various methodologies, but the very technological condition that *is discourse*, and which terms like ecology, economics, genetics, cosmology and cybernetics describe by facets. This is not to claim a privileged position for "technology," so-called, or related terms such as technē, technicity or technēsis, as some type of fetish or "paradigm of paradigms" around which all other discourses may be gathered, let alone as a "totalising" concept. Rather it is a question of recognising that today we remain confronted by a challenge that is a challenge to all critical discourses, and that is to think "concretely"—and with all the demands of a scientific rigour—alongside our various factographies, the structures of possibility that appear to underlie discourse in its supposed totality, and yet which open discourse to precisely the multiplicity of knowledges with which thinking is both enabled and circumscribed.

It is perhaps inevitable, that today more than ever it is the very status of the "human" that presents itself in various ways at the limits of theory. Even in the most technologically-orientated projects, we predictably find traces of humanism and metaphysics. As Arthur Bradley writes "the classic territory of the liberal humanist subject—mind, consciousness or agency—is still regarded as the privileged site for technological critique."[2] And if this remains the case after an already long history of scientific progressivism it is perhaps, as Giorgio Agamben has argued, "precisely because the human is already presupposed" every time we approach a thinking of technology. In the most primitive sense, thought itself is a type of "anthropological machine," yet this is not due to an immanence of reason (in man, in the world), but rather to what Agamben terms—not without ambiguity—a "state of exception" or "a zone of indeterminacy" produced by the machine; a state or zone which would correspond, in fact, to a generalised aporia "in which the outside is nothing but the exclusion of the inside and the inside is in turn only the inclusion of the outside." For Agamben, what this directly implies is that the anthropological machine is that which functions by excluding "as not (yet) human an already human being from itself."[3] Indeed, Agamben goes further and defines this movement of exclusion, which is also that of a recursion, as the "shadow of language."

Here, then, we have the delineations of a mode of thought that posits post-humanism as the very *field of invention* of the human. Where technology, as a series of mechanical artefacts, has nominally been seen to represent the estrangement or alienation of man, technology generalised as what Jean-François Lyotard calls the constelled structures of "intuitive, hypothetical configurations"[4]—

[2] Arthur Bradley, "Originary Technicity? Technology and Anthropology," *Technicity*, eds. Arthur Bradley and Louis Armand (Prague: Litteraria Pragensia, 2006) 80.
[3] Giorgio Agamben, "Anthropological Machine," *The Open: Man and Animal*, trans. Kevin Attell (Stanford: Stanford University Press, 2004) 37.
[4] Jean-François Lyotard, "Can Thought go without a Body?" trans. Bruce Boone and Lee Hildreth, *The Inhuman: Reflections on Time* (Stanford: Stanford University Press, 1991) 15.

in place of an "operativity" fixed in paradigms—describes an estrangement which is both conditional for a thinking of the human, but also an inhumanism which is the condition above all for technology.[5] Technology thus comes to be seen to function, as we see in Agamben,

> only by establishing a zone of indifference [...] within which—like a "missing link" which is always lacking because it is already virtually present—the articulation between human and animal, man and non-man, speaking being and living being [...]. Like every space of exception, this zone is, in truth, perfectly empty, and the truly human being who should occur there is only the place of a ceaselessly updated decision in which the caesurae and their rearticulation are always dislocated and displaced anew. What would thus be obtained, however, is neither an animal life nor a human life, but only a life that is separated and excluded from itself—only a bare life.[6]

This "only," this "bare" life, also implies an insufficiency, a minimum that nevertheless remains open, at its very core, to a movement of supplementarity. And it is to this movement that the "human" ultimately belongs and which brings about, at the same time as it necessarily abolishes its ground, the dualistic assumptions of a *"human life" or "animal life."* Indeed, this movement could be taken to describe an opening of finitude that extends even to what is, perhaps tautologically, referred to as "inorganic life." It is an insufficiency that is at one and the same time supplied in the efficiency of the supplement: of what Agamben, attempting to mediate this imaginary dualism, refers to as a "ceaselessly updated decision." A decision, moreover, that is nothing other than the event of "its own" aporia.

It is for this reason, perhaps, that Bernard Stiegler has come to argue that "technology is not, *and probably never has been*, a means for an end that would be science."[7] Nor, as Lyotard adds, is telechnology an objectification or "spatialising of meaning."[8] And if technology is taken to be the counterpart of a certain logotechnique, this would be because the limits of "human" thought are not simply consonant with what we call language systems, but are inscribed within the structures of "finitude" and "supplementarity" belonging to language and characteristic of its base potentiality. Signification and referentiality, in any case, will always have described a type of feedback loop, which effectively discounts the

---

[5] Lyotard, "Can Thought go without a Body?" 22-3.
[6] Agamben, "Anthropological Machine," 37-8.
[7] Cited in Lyotard, "*Logos* and *Technē*, or *Telegraphy*," *The Inhuman*, 47—emphasis added.
[8] Lyotard, "*Logos* and *Technē*," 47.

idea of a "posthumous thought" once the limits belonging to thought are recognised as "nothing other" than the "intuitive, hypothetical configurations" upon which technology devolves.

2. The Progress of Aporias

If, indeed, we are to credit the project of a generalised technicity in the theorising of structure, what would it mean to treat of a "residual anthropological dimension"[9] as an aporia of thinking the post-human, or indeed "inorganic life," if such an aporia is not also to be generalised in the problem of "experience" and "existence" — i.e. of bare life? The question is: how do we think the aporia of the so-called post-human otherwise? And this is a question about the means by which thinking comes, or may come, to touch upon the unthought—its modes of apprehension as such, its technai.

Such questions always pose a risk of a return to what Mark Hansen calls "formerly dominant conceptions" of technology, as either machine or text—wherever we treat a generalised technicity in theoretical, structural, or discursive terms.[10] It is important to note that the use of the term "discourse" here draws upon the character of discursus as dynamic structuration. What we call "language systems" (or texts) necessarily also partake of this sense of dynamic structure, and relate to the question of technicity in very much the same way Dürr's description of quantum mechanics relates other physical systems to "'information' without a carrier," or what Jacques Lacan elsewhere describes as "symbolic machines," linked to what Deleuze calls "machinic phylum." We must be vigilant, however, not to fall back upon the old machine aesthetics buoyed up by the duality of metaphor and materiality. Discourse is not taken here as a "mere metaphor" of so-called "material" technological change. Discourse is itself a physical system, and a τεχνολογέω, while materiality signifies a network of dynamic relations—which is what metaphor is.

It may be that, when we speak about technicity, we are in fact addressing what—within or framing a logic of technology, of prediction or of limits—remains structurally irresolvable. That the movement of thought is, in effect, that of a "progress of aporias." A progress by recursion, which describes fundamentally unmediated and unmediatable "relations"—thresholds, interstices, or singularities. What precisely the dynamics of this progress are to be, conceived in generalisable terms, remains in question. From a

9   Bradley, "Originary Technicity?" 79.
10   Mark Hansen, *Embodying Technesis: Technology beyond Writing* (Ann Arbor: University of Michigan Press, 2000).

system-scientific point of view, there is evidence to support the idea "that, in the neighbourhood of a singularity [...] a set of previously disconnected elements converges into a synergistic whole."[11] A complementary movement is often described in quantum mechanics, between superpositional states and observed states. Similar phenomena have been suggested in approaches to computational and cognitive linguistics — and in each case these sets or networks of relations may be said to be "transductive," where each relation constitutes its terms, and where "one term cannot precede the other because they exist only in relation."[12]

We may say that the progress of aporias in fact describes something like an evolutionary technē. This is already quite remote from ideas about so-called "global technicisation,"[13] let alone from the idea of a "purposive" technology as pure instrumentality. That is to say, remote from any deterministic view or any view that reduces technicity to a statement about means-ends. There is no "universal robotisation" or "gigantic, universal computer" lurking behind this evolutionary movement, guiding it like some sort of technicised éminence grise. As Jean-Luc Nancy has recently argued, such a determinism would presuppose "the resolution, in this computer, of what technology (taken absolutely) *is for*." For Nancy, technology *as such* remains "nothing other than the 'technique' of compensating for the nonimmanence of experience," so that whenever we speak of the "nexus" of technologies, or of technicity, what we are in fact speaking about is nothing more or less than "existing itself." Existing, as "the opening of finitude," is "technological through and through":

> Existence is not itself the technology of anything else, nor is technology "as such" the technology *of* existence: it is the "essential" technicity of existence insofar as *technology* has no essence and stands in for being.[14]

Here, then, the prosthetic character of technology is bound to existence in the form of a type of non-essentialised ontology. That is to say, of a fundamentally relational structure of "existence" whose operations, so to speak, are technologically orientated in the manner of, for example, a transduction. It is an orientation of the *non-*

[11] Manuel De Landa, *War in the Age of Intelligent Machine* (New York: Zone Books, 1991) 18.
[12] Stiegler, "The Discrete Image," 161. On transductive relations see particularly Gilbert Simondon, *Du mode d'existence des objets techniques* (Paris: Méot, 1958).
[13] Jean-Luc Nancy, *A Finite Thinking*, eds. Simon Sparks (Stanford: Stanford University Press, 2003) 26.
[14] Nancy, *A Finite Thinking*, 25.

immanent, whose "sense" obtains precisely in a progress of aporias. Nancy argues, "it is a matter of getting at the *sense* of 'technology' as the *sense* of existence." And it is also for this reason that we can say that "there *is* no technology 'as such,'" even while recognising that it is necessary to think beyond a simple "multiplicity of technologies."[15]

3. Technics or the Unthought?

"To 'inhabit' technology," Nancy suggests, "[...] would be nothing other than inhabiting and welcoming the finitude of sense."[16] If technology, which Nancy continues to speak of in the abstract while denying it in the "as such," implies specifically iterable and stochastic procedures, structures of supplementarity, recursion and supersession, and above all integrative and superpositional logics, then the very idea of finitude could be said to be bound up with whatever technology *is*. Or rather, whatever *sense* may be "attributable" to it (both transively and intransitively). And yet how do we speak of a sense of technology or even of a technological sense, without recourse to precisely the generalised discursivity that Nancy appears to reject as a "false concept," unless we are to trivialise it as simply a state of affairs—along the lines of "technology equals existence"? Perhaps what is really at issue here is the demand that we think technology differently—in parallel to a thinking of existence that is *no longer* that of an ontology. But this would require us firstly to address the possibility of joining (as Derrida says) the thinking of "the machine" and the thinking of "the event"[17]; and the possibility of establishing, *for* thinking, not simply the "limits" of thought, but the *status* of "the unthought."[18]

[15] Nancy, *A Finite Thinking*, 25-6.
[16] Nancy, *A Finite Thinking*, 25.
[17] Jacques Derrida, "Typewriter Ribbon: Limited Ink (2) ('within such limits')," trans. Peggy Kamuf, *Material Events: Paul de Man and the Afterlife of Theory*, eds. Tom Cohen, Barbara Cohen, J. Hillis Miller and Andrzej Warminski (Minneapolis: University of Minnesota Press, 2001) 335-6.
[18] If technology were to designate a type of "nothing," as Nancy at times suggests, then what would be the relation between the "sense" of technology and, for example, a technology *of the unthought*. Is "sense" here *nothing more* than a transduction: a discursive-technological event in the delimiting of the thinkable, or the signifiable, *as* thought or *as* signification? And is the *progress of aporias*—taken *as* thought—thus also an *impossible* thinking of the unthought, which is what philosophy and science have always attempted to practice behind the screen of categorisation and paradigmatics? Contrary to what Foucault has to say about this, the history of reason is *not* the history of an exclusion—the exclusion, for example, of the unthought in its various historical representations. Such things makes "no sense," in any case, and the very notion of an unthought entering into representation disqualifies it. The unthought, rather, is precisely what has always driven reason, and what allows reason to escape the determinability and totality that it has so often been painted as aspiring to—as

Such a task at times seems to recall us to the notion of something like a theoretical "unconscious"—an unthought which accompanies and underwrites the history of thought in ways that have not always been self-evident, but which may be likened to the event-state aporias envisaged by Dürr within the framework of quantum mechanics, and of those pertaining to the signifier-signified dichotomy in the semiological framework proposed by Saussure (and revealed in their broader complexity through the archival work of Johannes Fehr, particularly with regard to the seemingly contradictory status of "transmission" in Saussure's manuscripts). Yet this relation to an unthought would not be that of a simple binary opposition, but of the progress of aporias that underwrites and structures the binary relation "as such" as *dynamic interval*—whether phase transition, singularity or crisis point—in a global "language system." This system, as what Deleuze has called a "constellation of singularities," is fundamentally technological. In turn, each constellated structure evokes a type of "switching mechanism" (to return to the cybernetic metaphor of the circuit) in an overall event-state apparatus whose "existence" is not that of a *being for*—a resource, for example, that is posited by way of its availability for "work," as potentiality, latency or standing reserve—but of a generalised possibility, of a trans*duction* effect within what Dürr has termed "an indivisible, immaterial, temporally essentially undetermined network of relationships that determines only probabilities, differentiated capacity (potency) for a material-energetic realisation."[19]

The task of thinking technology differently—as here within a dynamic structural framework that is ostensibly that of a "language system," and not merely approximative of one—poses obvious questions for how, on the one hand, we theorise structure and how, on the other, structures may in turn be said to theorise.[20]

though the apotheosis of reason would be *nothing other* than the void. Indexed to the void, reason is not the concretisation of the unthought, of the event, of an origin, even of an originary différance or originary technicity. Such a void would still retain the character of a symbolic organisation, a *structure*, whether or not it is describable as a totality or a type of entropy, even as its indexicality points to what we might still call "the real." Which is to say, to the unthought *as such*. For this reason, among others, Nancy fails to recognise that it is *precisely* the assumption of being "indexed to the void"—or to "existence"—that technology, as Nancy calls it, invokes the final aporia which is that of the real itself, coded in the logic of indexicality, and substantiated in the claim upon a categorical "nothingness."

[19] Dürr, "Potsdamer Denkschrift," 3.

[20] Just as in the recent history of cybernetics and informatics we have moved from *models* of language, evolution and intelligence to interactual *prostheses* and hence to what may be called the *affective structures* of quantum computing, so to in the thinking of technology, the types of metaphysical or quasi-metaphysical categories invested in by a tradition stemming from Aristotle—i.e. of a technology "as such," of technē,

Just as Wittgenstein said that it is the hand that thinks, or Merleau-Ponty that it is the eye that is the "computer of being," so too we need to address technicity as other than simply the "irreducible multiplicity *of* technologies," as Nancy suggests, which "supplements *nothing*" or "compensates for a nonimmanence" that, also, is reducible to a "nothing."[21] Much more would need to be said about this, but at the very least we should ask about what makes possible the seemingly *affective structures* of technology that obtain both in relation to the human project and in distant remove from it, in the fundamental operations upon which the idea of "existence" devolves. Clearly, this is not a case for transcendence. Yet, it is also true, it is not a case of any "essence" of technology, although these operations may be "essentially" technological insofar as we are able to theorise them.

Louis Armand

---

even of technicity—increasingly come to submit to a logistics of generalisation that is no longer circumscribed by the progress of aporias (the limits of being, the opening of finitude, as Nancy says) but is rather evoked in the very *operations* of the aporia.
21 Nancy, *A Finite Thinking*, 24.

Note on the Text

With the exception of Benjamin H. Bratton's "Aesthetics of Logistics," Louis Armand's "Grammatica Speculativa" and Roy Ascott's "Terror Incognito" (which was presented at the "Mutamorphosis: Challenging Arts and Sciences" conference in Prague, 8-10 November 2007), all of the work collected in this volume was presented as part of the Prague "Frontiers of Theory" colloquium and the "Prague School and Theories of Structure" conference, which both took place at the Faculty of Philosophy, Charles University, 18-20 October 2007, within the framework of the international "Technicity" research project and under the joint auspices of the Czech Association for the Study of English (CZASE) and the European Thematic Network Project ACUME2: "Interfacing Science, Literature and the Humanities," co-ordinated by the University of Bologna. Particular thanks are due to Martin Procházka, Clare Wallace, David Vichnar, Roger Malina and Vita Fortunati.

Arthur Bradley

The Deconstruction of Christianity: On Touching the Frontiers of Theory

In recent years, the French philosopher Jean-Luc Nancy has begun to articulate something that he calls the "Deconstruction of Christianity" [*la Déconstruction du Christianisme*].[1] This project involves at least two distinct dimensions. On the one hand, Nancy seeks to show that the Christian tradition—for all its supposed complicity with metaphysics, ontotheology or logocentrism—is engaged in a process of auto-deconstruction: Christianity deconstructs itself [*ça se déconstruit*]. Yet this is only half the story. On the other hand, Nancy also seeks to argue that the post-Christian epoch—from the Enlightenment, through Marx, Nietzsche and Heidegger up to Derrida's own deconstruction—is a logical outworking of that same process of self-deconstruction: what we call deconstruction *itself* is inescapably Christian in origin. To Nancy's eyes, then, it would seem that the Deconstruction of Christianity necessitates an almost unimaginably huge re-writing of the past, present and more importantly the *future* of western thought. If Christianity is nothing other than a perpetual movement of self-overcoming, this means that everything we normally posit as "beyond" the Christian tradition— the Enlightenment, the "death" of God, the so-called "closure" of metaphysics and even the gesture of deconstruction itself—is inexorably re-absorbed back into it: "the world that is called modern is itself the becoming [*le devenir*] of Christianity" (*LD* 209). For Nancy, then, the Deconstruction of Christianity poses a critical

* This paper was originally delivered as a plenary lecture at the "Frontiers of Theory" colloquium on the 20th October 2007 at Charles University in Prague. I am extremely grateful to the organisers and participants of that colloquium and, in particular, Louis Armand, Stephen Dougherty, Christina Ljungberg, Laurent Milesi and Martin Procházka.

1 Jean-Luc Nancy, *La Déclosion: Déconstruction du christianisme 1* (Paris: Gallilee, 2005). All further references will be abbreviated in the text as *LD* followed by page number. Translations mine.

question to any allegedly secular, post-Christian philosophy. To what extent might the frontier of theory *still* be Christian?

It is equally possible, though, to pose this question back to Nancy himself. As Derrida has argued in his late work *On Touching*, the Deconstruction of Christianity risks making something of a Christianity of deconstruction. To be sure, Derrida concedes that Christianity can indeed be seen as a certain "deconstruction" *avant la lettre* even if that gesture obviously passes under other names: Christ's *kenosis*, *ascesis*, the mystical *hyperousios* and, particularly, the Lutheran act of *destructio*.[2] For Derrida, we should thus not be surprised to find that what we call "deconstruction" today retains the memory of Christianity within it: Luther's Protestant *destructio* of Catholic theology in order to return to the originary truth of scripture foreshadows Heidegger's *Destruktion* of the history of ontology in the name of a more original, Pre-Socratic experience of Being. However, "there is deconstruction and deconstruction," as Derrida puts it (*OT* 60), and here is the crux of his dispute with Nancy. If Nancy is surely right to say that we cannot simply step "beyond" Christianity — because the genius of Christianity is that it consists of nothing other than a series of steps beyond itself — Derrida believes that this insight is bought at the cost of a *hyperbolisation* of the Christian tradition: the overcoming [*dépassement*] of Christianity is always baptised in advance as a Christian self-overcoming [*auto-dépassement*]. In this sense, we might wonder whether Nancy presides over the re-Christianisation of western philosophy: "*All* our thought is Christian through and through" (*LD* 208-9).

Yet, if all this means that the Deconstruction of Christianity is a "difficult, paradoxical, almost impossible task" (*OT* 220), such "impossibility" is what famously drives any deconstruction worthy of the name. It is not Derrida's intention to simply rule out Nancy's project, so much as to put it to the test by trying to imagine what form it must — and must not — take. As with any act of deconstruction, a Deconstruction of Christianity must inhabit the Christian tradition from the inside: we can only begin to overcome Christianity by accepting our utter contamination by it. However, we accept tradition in order to reveal its essential non-identity with itself. What must be affirmed — and what Nancy himself does not sufficiently affirm — is that there is no single, self-identical or homogeneous "Christian tradition" in the first place. To put it an-

---

[2] Jacques Derrida, *On Touching—Jean-Luc Nancy*, trans. Christine Irizarry (Stanford: Stanford University Press, 2005) 59-60; 220. All further references will be abbreviated in the text as *OT*. The number of occasions where Derrida draws a parallel between Heidegger's *Destruktion* and Luther's *destructio* are almost too numerous to mention.

other way, the Deconstruction of Christianity is not so much a question of absorbing the entire history of the west into Christianity so much as *turning Christianity itself inside out*: Christianity must be exposed in its very interiority to an outside—a frontier— that is, if possible, even more exterior than the outside it has itself ceaselessly affirmed. For Derrida, in other words, the Deconstruction of Christianity must deconstruct the historical gesture of deconstruction that just *is* Christianity itself. If we are to focus upon just one such paradigmatic gesture of deconstruction within the Christian tradition, Derrida argues that it must be the Luthero-Heideggerian gesture of *destructio*: any Deconstruction of Christianity, he writes, must begin by "untying itself from a Christian tradition of *destructio*" whereby the act of self-deconstruction is part of an economy of self-sacrifice, self-purification and thus also self-preservation (*OT* 60). In that sense, what emerges from the other side of this process cannot simply be a more originary, purer "Christianity."

What, though, might this Deconstruction of Christianity look like? I think there are many possible answers to this question— Judaism and Islam to name only the most obvious!—but in what follows I want to propose just one. To introduce my own argument, I want to suggest that the Deconstruction of Christianity might take the form of a new continental philosophy of *technology*. It is one of the major axioms of recent continental thought (Derrida, Lyotard, the work of Bernard Stiegler and, of course, the Nancy of *Corpus*) that what we call the "human" is neither a biological entity (a body, a gene-carrier, a species) nor a philosophical state (a soul, mind or consciousness) but something whose "nature" exists in relation to technological prostheses. According to a logic that will be very familiar to readers of Derrida's work, technology is a supplement that exposes an originary *lack* within what should be the integrity or propriety of the human being itself.[3] For Derrida, in other words, humanity is constituted not by any positive essence, being or substance but by a relation to what ostensibly lies beyond it: we "are," so to speak, our own outside [*pro-thesis*]. If this philosophy of technology seems alien to the history, dogma and traditions of Christianity, Derrida suggests in a remarkable footnote to *On Touching* that it represents a mode of deconstruction that "distances itself from the (Luthero-Heideggerian) *destructio*" which is specifically identified as, and with, Christianity (*OT* 345 n26). In other words, the deconstruction of the body fulfils *the very criteria*

---

[3] Jacques Derrida, *Of Grammatology*, trans. Gayatri Chakravorty Spivak (Baltimore: Johns Hopkins University Press) 244.

Derrida sets earlier in the book for a new Deconstruction of Christianity.

To flesh out this point a little more, I want to focus on just one thread in the complex tapestry of arguments that is *On Touching*: the critique of Husserl, Merleau-Ponty, Franck and Chrétien's phenomenology of touch in Part 2 of that work. It might well seem odd at first to use phenomenology as a means of pursuing a Deconstruction of Christianity but in many ways this is precisely Derrida's point: Husserl and his successors are—for all the supposed scientific rigour of the *epochē*—by no means exterior to the Christian metaphysical tradition. On the contrary, the phenomenology of touch—which privileges tactility above all other senses as the most direct and unmediated form of intuition—belongs to a Christian tradition of valorising the body that can be traced all the way back to the Incarnation: the Christian *corpus* or body consists in nothing other than a certain thinking *of* the body. However, the intention here is not merely to demonstrate Nancy's point about the inescapability of the Christian legacy (even or especially by modernity) so much as to expose the fact that there is no one, single, homogenous Christian "legacy." For Derrida, once again, the Deconstruction of the Christian origins of phenomenology is not just another way of showing that "everything is always already Christian" but a way of showing how in its very "interiority" Christianity is exposed to what lies beyond it. In "Hand of God, Hand of Man," what lies beyond/within Christianity is a certain technical or prosthetic logic that is the very condition of the (Christian) body: the apparent immediacy, continuity and indivisibility of the touch is always mediated by and through an other.

For Derrida, this critique of the Christian history of the phenomenology of touch—of phenomeno-theology— takes the form of a sustained and remarkable reflection on the place of the *hand*. What exactly *is* a hand? Who or what does the *hand* belong to— animal, man, god? Why, in particular, does the history of phenomenology from Husserl, through Heidegger and Merleau-Ponty, up to contemporary figures like Franck and Chrétien accord such a massive privilege to the hand as the condition of all tactility? Let me briefly trace our answers to these questions:

1. To start with, we need merely note the absolute indispensability of the hand to the foundational texts of 20th-century phenomenology. As Derrida shows, Husserl's *Ideas II* are remarkable for the enormous stress they place upon touch: tactility is not merely one sense amongst others but the fundamental condition of our relation both to our own bodies and to our life-world. For Husserl, the privileged means of this tactile relation is the hand: what may at first seem to be a mere appendage is in fact the sign

of our existence as free, willing, spontaneous, affecting and auto-affecting egos (*OT* 160). More generally, the hand is also the index of a metaphysics of immediate, intuitive presence whether it be of our own bodies or of the world: the finger that touches something is simultaneously and indivisibly touched *by* that something in a way that applies for no other sense. (We will have plenty to say about the obvious metaphysics of this idea of the touch later on.) In 20th-century phenomenology, this valorisation of the hand persists—beginning of course with Heidegger's own paradigmatic attempt to articulate *Dasein*'s engagement with the world through the concept of the "ready-to-hand" (*Zuhandenheit*).

2. Yet, what none of this tells us is *why* the hand is so indispensable to the history of phenomenology. It may well be that tactility is the most direct and immediate form of intuition—though Derrida will locate problems here too—but none of this explains why the *hand* alone is deemed the privileged or exclusive vehicle of touch: where does this leave the rest of the body, the mouth, the genitalia and so on—are they not capable of touch? More to the point, what about those bodies that do not possess hands but claws, paws and so on—are human beings really the *only* beings that are capable of touch, and thus a relation to their own bodies and to the world? Of course, Husserl does not quite say this and there are good phenomenological grounds for focusing an analysis upon human beings rather than animals: we should always begin with the being that is closest to us and nothing is closer than the being that we ourselves are (*OT* 166-7). Even so, a rigorous phenomenology should suspend all reference to the real nature of both the perceiver and the perceived—the "who" and the "what"—and concentrate on the phenomenon alone, and there are grounds for wondering whether this is really the case here. Just as Husserl's phenomenology of the sign fails to bracket off a certain metaphysics of the voice, so his phenomenology of touch is contaminated by a metaphysical anthropology. For Derrida, that is, what is at stake in the phenomenology of the hand is a residual anthropocentrism that establishes a rigid hierarchy and teleology: the only being that can genuinely touch—and thus constitute himself as free, spontaneous agent—is man (*OT* 154).

3. We can go further. As Derrida goes on to argue, what we are dealing with here is not simply an anthropology but a *theology*: the phenomenology of touch—continuous, immediate and indivisible—inevitably touches upon a theology of touch, of contact, of consubstantiality of being that finds its paradigmatic example in the doctrine of the Incarnation. To prove this—somewhat risky—point,

Derrida turns to Jean-Louis Chrétien's phenomenology of the "hand of god."[4] On one level, of course, nothing could be further from the scientific rigour of Husserl than this kind of phenomenological theology: it is no surprise that Chrétien was, along with Jean-Luc Marion and Michel Henry, the principal target of Dominique Janicaud's polemic against the "*tournant theologique*" in French phenomenology.[5] Nonetheless, we can draw a direct line from the metaphysics of the touch in Husserl's *Ideas II* to the theology of the touch in Chrétien's *L'appel et la réponse*. For Chrétien, it is only when we are touched by the *divine* that we achieve the full, immediate and intuitive plenitude promised by Husserl: only the hand of god genuinely delivers up the spatial and temporal presence offered by the hand of man. If we commonly think of the "hand of god" as nothing more than a metaphor or analogy drawn from the sensible, finite hand of man, in other words, Chrétien turns this logic on its head: it is the hand of man that is a figure for the real, authentic and immediate touch offered by the hand of god. Now, this is not to say that Chrétien simply *opposes* the philosophical privilege accorded to human touch above all others because what defines the spiritual touch for him is precisely the doctrine of the Incarnation, that is to say, the becoming-human of the spiritual. Rather, we might say that the hand of god is paradoxically the only means of ensuring the historical privilege accorded to the hand of man: it is the hand of god that *gives* the hand of man, that *reveals itself to* that hand and *redeems* it from its creaturely finitude. So, the historical excellence of the human hand is preserved as that which is called by, and responds to, the spiritual touch of the Incarnation.

In all these senses, we might wonder whether Chrétien's analysis of the "hand of god" does not so much represent a "theological turn" in phenomenology (*à la* Janicaud) but rather the final outworking of the anthropo-theological assumptions that have *always* been in play in discussions of the human hand: Christianity deconstructs itself in order to re-appear as the phenomeno-theology of touch.

What form, though, might a *deconstruction* of this Christian phenomenology of touch take? It is, once again, a question neither of opposing that history from some spurious exterior position, nor of hyperbolising it, but of exposing its own "outside" within it: the anthropotheological hand is not at one with itself. As Derrida tantalisingly suggests, it is possible to offer an *other* history of the hand

---

4   Jean-Louis Chrétien, *L'appel et la réponse* (Paris: Minuit, 1992).
5   Dominique Janicaud, et al, *Le tournant théologique de la phénoménologie française* (Paris: L'Eclat, 1991).

that exists independently of all anthropotheology: the "history of the hand" remains "impossible to dissociate" from the "history of technics" he writes (*OT* 154). Let me conclude by briefly teasing out some of the implications of this position:

1. To Derrida's way of thinking, as we have already seen, it is clear that a certain technicity—mediation, spacing or substitutability—always exists at the heart of the phenomenology of touch. Of course, we can again trace this critique back to the very beginning of his philosophy: what *Speech and Phenomena* did for the metaphysics of speech, *On Touching* now does for contact. As we move from Husserl, through Merleau-Ponty, all the way up to Nancy's own discussions of the plasticity of the body in *Corpus*, we find that mediation always insinuates itself between the apparent spatio-temporal immediacy of contact: there is a spatio-temporal difference even between the simultaneity of the touching and the touched. Why is this? For Derrida, we might go so far as to say that the "phenomenology of touch" is, even on its own terms, an oxymoron: what makes it possible for us to analyse touch as a *phenomenon*—the reduction or bracketing of the world in all its contingency, variability and changeability—is precisely what forbids any *real* experience of contact itself. The phenomenon of contact—with all the immediacy, simultaneity and presence it entails and guarantees—is only constituted on the basis of the suspension of real contact. In this essential mediation that constitutes our very experience of the immediate, the originary technicity of perception, affection and auto-affection is born: "what calls for "technics," then, is the phenomenological necessity itself" (*OT* 230).

2. Perhaps we can best witness this technicity in operation by returning to the question that drives Derrida's entire discussion. To recall: what exactly *is* a "hand"? Who does it belong to? Where does it come from? As we have seen, anthropotheology provides one answer to that question: the hand is the hand *of* man—the hand that defines man as man and not animal, the hand that enables him to touch himself and his world, the hand that guarantees his privileged status as free, spontaneous, self-moving, affecting and auto-affecting ego. However, there is another history of the hand, and another Deconstruction of Christianity, albeit one that is only alluded to by Derrida himself in the footnotes to the text (*OT* 345 n26; 362 n34), but one that I would like to tease out here. For the French palaeo-anthropologist André Leroi-Gouhran—whose ground-breaking work is discussed by Derrida as early as the *Grammatology* and referred to once again in the notes to *On Touching*—the hand is the engine that drives the process of

hominisation itself: the birth of the hand is the birth of the human.[6] Quite simply, Leroi-Gourhan argued that the post-war discovery of prehominid remains that were upright, bipedal and tool-using, but which nonetheless possessed very limited brain capacity, required a complete re-writing of the story of human evolution: what we call the brain was not the *cause* of tool-use, language and so on, but the *effect*. The attainment of an upright posture by prehominid man freed the hands for tool use, which, in turn, liberated the lower jaw for language and enabled the cerebral cortex to develop to a position where it was capable of symbolic thought. This means that what makes human beings "human" in the first place is not consciousness, intelligence and so on but precisely our relation to the allegedly non-human world of technicity. In Leroi-Gouhran's account, the site of this originary interface between the human and the non-human is the *hand*.

3. What, then, *is* a hand? In Leroi-Gouhran's view, we can give a radically different and more surprising answer to that supplied by the history of anthropotheology: the hand is not the guarantee of immediacy so much as the first *mediation*. It is what we might paradoxically call a "natural" or original prosthesis—an exteriorisation that constitutes the interior of our body. To put it another way, the hand of man evolves in a reciprocal relation with the technical implements it wields. On the one side, of course, the hand *shapes* the environment around it into a tool or instrument: the very act of picking up a twig in order to dig in the earth transforms that twig into a technical implement. On the other side, though, the hand is *shaped by* the environment into a kind of meta-tool, a tool-using tool: the act of picking up a twig requires a gripper with independent digits, opposable thumbs, that is, *another* technical implement. For Bernard Stiegler, whose monumental study *La technique et le temps* is heavily indebted to Leroi-Gouhran, what all this makes possible is the recognition of the *co-evolution* of the human and the technical: "the human inventing the technical, the technical inventing the human" across history.[7] More radically still, the technical history of the hand proposed by Leroi-Gouhran also calls into question the anthropological privilege accorded to the human by Christianity and, latterly, the phenomenology of touch. If phenomenology speaks of the hand of *man*—the hand as the sign, attribute and extension of a pre-existing human being who occupies pole position in a teleological

---

[6] André Leroi-Gouhran, *Le geste et la parole: la mémoire et les rythmes* (Paris: Albin Michel, 1964).

[7] Bernard Stiegler, *Technics and Time 1: The Fault of Epimetheus*, trans. Richard Beardsworth and George Collins (Stanford: Stanford University Press, 1998) 127.

hierarchy—the philosophy of technology turns that logic inside out and forces us to speak of what we might call the man of *hand*: the human race possesses no positive substance—a soul, free will, or consciousness—because it is constituted through and through by its relation to technical prostheses. The relation to technology is what constitutes the human, then, but humanity cannot claim even this bare relation as a defining or exclusive property. This capacity to make and use tools is also possessed by a wide range of species—most notably, but not just, large primates—that do not possess the human hand.[8] So, what becomes of *homo faber* when man is not the only maker?

In other words, what appears to be most proper to the human's privileged relation to, and within, the world—to constitute our privileged status within the world as free, spontaneous, (self-)affecting egos—is in fact that which utterly *ex-propriates* the human: our experience of ourselves is always mediated because *the very agency of that self-experience*—the hand—is *itself* a medium.

What is the meaning of this insight? It has been my hypothesis that the Deconstruction of the body is also and at the same stroke a Deconstruction of Christianity: a body that is "originally and essentially open to the *technē*" is also one that is involved in a "'deconstruction of Christianity,' of the Christian body, a deconstruction of Christian 'flesh'" (*OT* 218-19). Everything hinges upon the fact that the phenomenology of touch is inseparable from a Christian theology of immediacy, of plenitude, of consubstantiality and ultimately incarnation. Such, at least, is the wager on which *On Touching* stakes itself: we would have no phenomenon of touch—no concept of the spatio-temporal identity between the touching and the touched—without Christianity. Yet, if Christianity tells us that the hand of man always contains within it a real, divine presence, I have tried to show that the philosophy of technology turns that hand inside out, like the fingers of a glove, exposing the exteriority, mediation, technicity from which it is stitched. To put it another way, the hand exists not in order to touch without mediation but because *there is no* touch, no immediacy: it touches upon what is essentially and irreducibly *untouchable*, that is to say the unmediated experience of touch itself. Let me conclude by sketching three of the larger areas of enquiry for this Deconstruction of Christianity and thus, for theories of technology more generally:

---

8   See W.C. McGrew, *Chimpanzee Material Culture: Implications for Human Evolution* (Cambridge: Cambridge University Press, 1992) for an excellent survey of the larger implications of primate tool use.

1. Firstly, I think that the philosophy of technology necessitates a radical—yet reading of the history of religion as part of the evolution of technical prostheses. It is becoming increasingly urgent, as Derrida puts it in the essay "Faith and Knowledge" to think "faith" and the "machine-like" together as one and the same possibility and we can detect similar moves in the recent work of Régis Debray and Bernard Stiegler.[9] What, to take only the crudest question, are the technological conditions—language, alphabetic writing, scrolls, effigies, idols and icons, the printing press, virtual media and, less positivistically, what Derrida calls the trace—that make faith, religion, the (apparently unscathed or unmediated) experience of the *sacred* itself both possible and impossible?[10]

2. We also have to consider the implications of the philosophy of originary technicity for our ethical, political and religious present. It is now something of a cliché to speak of how new scientific and technological advances—artificial intelligence, the mapping of the human genome, advances in genetic engineering are challenging our idea of "what it means to be human": *zoē*, *bios*, rational animal, *homo faber*, *homo sapiens*, *Dasein*. To be sure, the work of Foucault and Agamben on the bio-political is an indispensable reference point here but perhaps—as Derrida indicates in that one famous and rather damning reference to Agamben in *Rogues*—we need to go further still.[11] If human beings exist solely in relation to technological prostheses—if our body is *itself* a kind of originary prosthesis—then this transforms the entire terms of the debate: the bio-politicisation of life is merely the logical outworking of *an originary contamination of biology and politics*, a political ontology, that just is life itself. Who—or what—will constitute or safeguard the anthropotheological sanctity of "life" in the radical *absence* of any defining human essence or existence?

3. Finally, and to go back to where we started, what remains is the question of the *future* of Christianity itself, and, with it, the frontier of theory. We began by asking whether it is possible to think a "beyond" of this most plastic, self-exceeding and self-

---

[9] See Bernard Stiegler, "Derrida and Technology: Fidelity at the Limits of Deconstruction and the Prosthesis of Faith," trans. Richard Beardsworth in *Jacques Derrida and the Future of the Humanities*, ed. Tom Conley (Cambridge: Cambridge University Press, 2002) 238-70; and Régis Debray *God: An Itinerary*, trans. Jeffrey Mehlman (London: Verso, 2004).

[10] See Jacques Derrida, "Faith and Knowledge: The Two Sources of 'Religion' within the Limits of Reason Alone," trans. Samuel Weber in *Religion*, eds. Jacques Derrida and Gianni Vattimo (London: Polity, 1998) 1-78.

[11] See Jacques Derrida, *Voyous: deux essais sur la raison* (Paris: Galilée, 2003) 46. In one of the very few references to Agamben anywhere in his work, Derrida argues that the opposition between *zoē* and *bios* that operationalises Agamben's theory of biopolitics represents a deeply reductive reading of the Aristotelian concept of life.

deconstructing of traditions—without falling into the twin traps of either accepting it uncritically or reproducing it in secularised form under the pretence of overcoming it. Quite simply, what is at stake here is what is at stake throughout Derrida's work from beginning to end: the affirmation of an absolute other that is irreducible to every horizon of expectation whether it be a messianic dogma or a techno-scientific calculation. If the philosophy of technology is indeed a Deconstruction of Christianity, what is crucial is that it must not merely *repeat* (whether wittingly or unwittingly) the historic self-deconstructions of Christianity itself. Perhaps we might go further still. To what extent, although this is a question for another day, might technicity—which after Heidegger is almost exclusively, but now very reductively, associated with pure calculability, anticipation and the foreclosure of the future—actually constitute a more powerful way of *affirming* the radical, non-teleological openness of futurity than is elsewhere called the messianic?[12]

In each case, the task of going beyond Christianity will always be to think "substitution *without* sacrifice," deconstruction without *destructio*, an emptiness emptier than the *kenosis* through which Christianity has always re-filled itself (*OT* 262). Such, perhaps, would be a Deconstruction of Christianity that did not make a Christianity of Deconstruction.

[12] See Arthur Bradley, "Derrida's god: A Genealogy of the Theological Turn," *Paragraph* 29.3 (2006): 21-42 for a first tentative attempt to address this question.

Laurent Milesi

Almost Nothing at the Beginning: The Technicity of the Trace in Deconstruction

Although this paper neither intends nor pretends to offer a genealogy of the Derridean "quasi-concept" of the trace—notably its relation to Martin Heidegger's *frühe Spur*, the originary difference between Being and beings lost in the history of metaphysics, to Emmanuel Levinas's more ethical trace of the Other,[1] or to the phenomenological (Husserlian) tradition[2]—I would like to start with some contextual reminders in order to frame the project behind the title within a dual articulation of the Derridean trace. A companion piece, commissioned for a special issue of the *Oxford Literary Review* on "Derridanimals," had focused on its joint dimension of animality which, together with technicity, extends the functioning of the classical "trace" beyond (and before) its human register.[3] Highlighting this double facet of the "originarily" nonhuman trace and summarising the latter's trajectory through key stages in Der-

---

[1] Derrida mentions Levinas's "La Trace de l'autre" in "Violence and Metaphysics," *Writing and Difference*, trans. Alan Bass (London: Routledge and Kegan Paul, 1978) 118. See also 396 n1, referring to its concomitant publication and 412 n92, which quotes from it.

[2] See especially Jacques Derrida et al., *Edmund Husserl's "Origin of Geometry": An Introduction*, new ed., trans., with preface and afterword, by John P. Leavey, Jr. (Lincoln: University of Nebraska Press, 1989); and, for a recent critical articulation, Paola Marrati, *Genesis and Trace: Derrida Reading Husserl and Heidegger*, trans. Simon Sparks (Stanford: Stanford University Press, 2005). See also Tim Herrick, "'A book which is no longer discussed today': Tran Duc Thao, Jacques Derrida, and Maurice Merleau-Ponty," *Journal of the History of Ideas* 66.1 (2005): 127, who notes a terminological similarity with Merleau-Ponty's use of the word.

[3] See Laurent Milesi, "Saint-Je Derrida," forthcoming in a special issue of the *Oxford Literary Review* on "Derridanimals," ed. Neil Badmington. The constitutive animality of the Derridean trace was developed there in relation to autobiography as "the trace of the living for itself"—"The Animal That Therefore I Am (More to Follow)," trans. David Wills, *Critical Inquiry* 28 (2002): 415—and "mimēsis."

rida's oeuvre will also enable me to address the critique formulated by Bernard Stiegler but also, among others, by Richard Beardsworth and Arthur Bradley, of the alleged ahistorical ideality and residual anthropocentrism of Derrida's understanding of technicity.

1. The trace as animal trail/track

In *L'Animal que donc je suis* Derrida recalled that his understanding of (arche-)writing had always been linked, from its inception, to that of the effacement of an animal trace, within a critique of the neutralisation or forgetting by anthropologocentrism of the "zoic" origin of the *logos*: "The mark, the gram, the trace, différance [i.e. four in a chain of nonsynonymous, substitutable quasi-concepts[4]], concern differentially all the living, all the relations of the living to the nonliving."[5] Several pages before, Derrida had defined animality, the life of the living, as a "spontaneity [...] to [...] marking, tracing, and affecting itself with traces of its self."[6] Indeed, as early as "Freud and the Scene of Writing," one can read for instance that "Life must be thought of as trace before Being may be determined as presence."[7] And even before the explicit interweavings of *trace*, *tracé* and *tracement*, across "graphies" and tracks, in "Différance" and more generally the complexification of the border between animality and humanity in *Margins of Philosophy*, *Of Grammmatology* had stated that the trace, which "[a]rticulat[es] the living upon the nonliving in general," "arche-phenomenon of 'memory,' [...] must be thought before the opposition of [...] animality and humanity," soon after expressing an affinity with Levinas's (but also Nietzsche's, Freud's and Heidegger's) conception of the trace, within the critique of ontology, as "relationship to the illeity as to the alterity of a past that never was and can never

4   Cf. Jacques Derrida, "Différance," *Margins of Philosophy*, trans. Alan Bass (Brighton: Harvester, 1982) 12: "Now if we consider the chain in which *différance* lends itself to a certain number of nonsynonymous substitutions, according to the necessity of the context, why have recourse to the 'reserve,' to 'archi-writing,' to the 'archi-trace,' to 'spacing,' that is, to the 'supplement,' or to the *pharmakon*, and soon to the hymen, to the margin-mark-march, etc." To this list, "dissemination," "graft" and "parergon" are added in *Positions*, trans. and annotated by Alan Bass (London: Continuum, 2002 [1981]) 41.

5   Jacques Derrida, *L'Animal que donc je suis*, ed. Marie-Louise Mallet (Paris: Galilée, 2006) 144—translation mine. This text was first given as a ten-hour address at the Cerisy-la-Salle *décade* on "L'Animal autobioghraphique" in July 1997, and the first part published initially in the proceedings volume, *L'Animal autobiographique. Autour de Jacques Derrida*, ed. Marie-Louise Mallet (Paris: Galilée, 1999) 251-303.

6   Derrida, "The Animal That Therefore I Am (More to Follow)," 417.

7   Derrida, *Writing and Difference*, 255.

be lived in the originary or modified form of presence."[8] The animality of the trace is even clearly foregrounded in the second part, on Rousseau: "We must begin wherever we are and the thought of the trace, which cannot not take the scent [*flair*] into account, has already taught us that it was impossible to justify a point of departure absolutely."[9] In-between these two diametrically opposed works in time, "Mes Chances" had reiterated that the replacement of signifier, letter or word by mark or trace was strategically meant to point beyond the linguistic sign as essentially human.[10]

Distantly redeploying the "logic of obsequence" first developed in *Glas*, the *"Je le suis à la trace"* ventured later in *H.C. pour la vie, c'est à dire...*,[11] formulaically works against ontological antecedence but also neutralises Heidegger's residual anthropologocentric ontology, his denial of being and *logos* to the animal also glimpsed in *Aporias*. Or again, in the words of *L'Animal que donc je suis*: *"Ecce animot*: that is the announcement of which I am (following) something like the trace, assuming the title of an autobiographical animal, in the form of a risky, fabulous, or chimerical response to the question: 'But me, who am I?'"[12]

2. The arche-trace as erasure

Whether as mark, gram or trace, taken in metonymic substitution as the production of *différance*, the Derridean trace is by structural necessity constituted by erasure: "An unerasable trace is not a

[8] Jacques Derrida, *Of Grammatology*, rev. ed., trans. Gayatri Chakravorty Spivak (Baltimore: Johns Hopkins University Press, 1997 [1967]) 65; 70, which further states about this new proposed science that it "ought not to be *one of the sciences of man*, because it asks first, as its characteristic question, the question of the *name of man*" (83). On the same page, Gelb's *A Study of Writing*, which had first ventured the word "grammatology," is famously recalled and praised; cf. I.J. Gelb, *A Study of Writing*, rev. ed. (Chicago: University of Chicago Press, 1963 [1952]) 23: "The aim of this book is to lay a foundation for a full science of writing, yet to be written. To the new science we could give the name 'grammatology,' following partially the term 'grammatography' which was used some years ago in the title of a book on writing published in England [Friedrich Ballhorn's 1861 study, originally in German, in which this specific word was not used, however]." Though Derrida's "science of the effacement of the trace" (*Of Grammatology*, xlviii) would never call itself a "full" science of writing, it was likewise to be understood as a science-to-come within this "project."

[9] Derrida, *Of Grammatology*, 162.

[10] Jacques Derrida, "My Chances / *Mes Chances*: A Rendezvous with Some Epicurean Stereophonies," trans. Irene Harvey and Avital Ronell; *Taking Chances: Derrida, Psychoanalysis, and Literature*, eds. Joseph H. Smith and William Kerrigan (Baltimore: Johns Hopkins University Press, 1984) 16. Cf. also *L'Animal que donc je suis*, 185.

[11] Jacques Derrida, *H.C. pour la vie, c'est à dire...* (Paris: Galilée, 2002) 89; cf. *H.C. for Life, That Is to Say...*, trans., with additional notes, by Laurent Milesi and Stefan Herbrechter (Stanford: Stanford University Press, 2007) 101-2.

[12] Derrida, "The Animal That Therefore I Am (More to Follow)," 416.

trace."[13] Towards the end of the last section of "Ousia and Grammē" ("The Closure of the Grammē and the Trace of Difference"), while recalling the passage on the lost "early trace" in Heidegger's "Anaximander Fragment,"[14] Derrida expands as follows, reworking an earlier development in the "Différance" section similarly featuring a (fuller) commentary on the erasure of the originary trace of difference between Being and beings according to Heidegger:

> The trace of difference is erased. If one recalls that difference (is) itself other than absence and presence, (is) (itself) trace, it is indeed the trace of the trace that has disappeared in the forgetting of the difference between Being and beings.
> [...]
> But at the same time, this erasure of the text must have been traced in the metaphysical text. Presence, then, far from being, as is commonly thought, *what* the sign signifies, what a trace refers to [...], is the trace of the trace, the trace of the erasure of the trace.[15]

The erasure of the early trace (*die frühe Spur*) of difference is therefore the "same" as its tracing in the text of metaphysics. This latter must have maintained the mark of what it has lost, reserved, put aside. The paradox of such a structure, in the language of metaphysics, is an inversion of metaphysical concepts, which produces the following effect: the present becomes the sign of the sign, the trace of the trace. It is no longer what every reference refers to in the last analysis. It becomes a function in a structure of generelised reference. It is a trace, and a trace of the erasure of the trace.[16]

Or, as Rodolphe Gasché neatly summarises:

> for Derrida, the word ["trace"] designates something of which the metaphysical concepts of trace and presence are the erasure. From Derrida's analysis of Heidegger's concept of *die frühe Spur*, it follows that trace is the necessarily metaphysical concept that names an originary tracing and effacement, of which the traditional conceptual dyad of trace and presence within the metaphysical text is the trace of effacement [...].[17]

---

[13] Derrida, *Writing and Difference*, 289, 336.

[14] Martin Heidegger, "The Anaximander Fragment," *Early Greek Philosophy*, trans. David Farrell Krell and Frank Capuzzi (New York: Harper and Row, 1975), especially 50: "The oblivion of Being is oblivion of the difference between being and beings."

[15] Derrida, *Margins of Philosophy*, 65-66.

[16] Derrida, *Margins of Philosophy*, 24.

[17] Rodolphe Gasché, *The Tain of the Mirror: Derrida and the Philosophy of Reflection* (Cambridge, Mass: Harvard University Press, 1986) 186 (see also *passim* in the subsections on "The Infrastructure as Arche-Trace" and "The Infrastructure as Différance" [186-205]). See also his *Inventions of Difference: On Jacques Derrida* (Cambridge, Mass: Harvard University Press, 1994) especially 45.

Reinscribing or re-marking the metaphysical concept, the Derridean "trace" (arche-trace) is always already the trace of a trace[18] as it is affected by the structure of doubling and deferral in the work of *différance* as tempor(al)isation. Its originary effacement will be repeated in the iterative drama of hierarchised differences according to a structure of delay or *Nachträglichkeit* that makes it akin to the Freudian-Lacanian trauma as the repetition of what never was.[19] The tropic turn within the structure of (effacement or erasure) of the trace is thus to be understood as the disappearance of the origin which did not even disappear:

It is not absence instead of presence, but a trace which replaces a presence which has never been present, an origin by means of which nothing has begun.[20]

The trace is not only the disappearance of origin—within the discourse that we sustain and according to the path that we follow it means that the origin did not even disappear, that it was never constituted except reciprocally by a nonorigin, the trace, which thus becomes the origin of the origin. From then on, to wrench the concept of the trace from the classical scheme, which would derive it from a presence or from an originary nontrace and which would make of it an empirical mark, one must indeed speak of an originary trace or arche-trace. Yet we know that that concept destroys its name and that, if all begins with the trace, there is above all no originary trace.[21]

Following the double semantics of the Latin *re-*,[22] this "bending-back of a return" (cf. "reciprocally"), or "movement of repetition,"[23] of the (arche-)trace as the origin of all relation to an Other

---

18 Cf. also Derrida's interview "Semiology and Grammatology" in *Positions*, 24 (see 7-8; 23-26; 37-41 on trace and *différance*), and Gasché, *Inventions of Difference*, 44-49 (on the arche-trace).

19 See Derrida, *Margins of Philosophy*, 21.

20 Derrida, *Writing and Difference*, 372.

21 Derrida, *Of Grammatology*, 61. Cf. also Gasché, *The Tain of the Mirror*, 188.

22 See Gasché, *The Tain of the Mirror*, 225, who adduces re-mark, re-trait, and *restance* among other examples.

23 Jacques Derrida, *Speech and Phenomena, and Other Essays on Husserl's Theory of Signs*, trans. David B. Allison (Evanston, IL: Northwestern University Press, 1973) 68. Looking at the common root between retention and re-presentation or protention in Husserl's conception of consciousness, Derrida equates "the possibility of re-petition in its most general form" with "the constitution of a trace in the most universal sense," and further notes the primordiality of the iterable trace which "not only must inhabit the pure actuality of the now but must constitute it through the very movement of difference it introduces" (67). If there is ideality, it is in the form of presence insofar as the latter is predicated upon the—we may add: *material*—inscription in presence itself of an infinite re-petition, re-turn *ad infinitum*, as a return of the same. Hence, in "Différance," the following Husserlian definition: "And it is this constitution of the present, as an "originary" and irreducibly nonsimple (and therefore, *stricto*

(Levinas), of temporality (Husserl), and of language and sense (Saussure),[24] as (lack of) originary trace or as the origin of the origin, makes the reinscribed trace a "pre-originary" (also, as we saw, pre-ontological), prosthetic supplement which, like technology for Stiegler, exposes the originarily constitutive lack within the human—what the latter, in his major ongoing project *Technics and Time*, calls the de-fault (*le défaut qu'il faut*) or lack in the organic at the origin, inflecting Heidegger's "being-at-fault" (*Schuldigsein*) in *Being and Time*.[25] I will return later to the prosthetics of this double operation in *re-* at the core of the technical trace, but also "trait," first in the light of Derrida's essay on "The Retrait of Metaphor," and finally as the "desistential" operation of *restance*.

3. The techno-poiesis of the arche-trace

In his epoch-making essay translated as "The Question Concerning Technology" (1955), Heidegger famously inquired into the "essence" of technology, within a critique of the metaphysics of presence, as a "way" of revealing or unconcealing the totality of Being. Uncovering art's lost, forgotten etymological kinship to it already announced in "The Origin of the Work of Art" (1935-36), Heidegger states once more, undoing Plato's celebrated opposition in *Timaeus*: "*Technē* belongs to bringing-forth, to *poiēsis*; it is something poetic [*Poietisches*]."[26] I wish to recall this forgotten techno-poietic *archē* according to Heidegger as the linkage between writing and technology can be extended to Derrida's insistent equation between writing and trace, even though, in the roughly contemporaneous words of *Of Grammatology*, "[w]riting is one of the representatives of the trace, it is not the trace itself."[27] Hence the quasi-substitutability of arche-witing and the arche-trace,

sensu nonoriginary) synthesis of marks, or traces of retentions and protentions [...], that I propose to call archi-writing, archi-trace or *différance*: Which (is) (simultaneously) spacing (and) temporalisation." (*Margins of Philosophy*, 13).

[24] Derrida, *Of Grammatology*, 47: "The general structure of the unmotivated trace connects within the same possibility, and they cannot be separated except by abstraction, the structure of the relationship with the other, the movement of temporalisation, and language as writing." Cf. also Gasché, *Inventions of Différence*, 45-46.

[25] See Bernard Stiegler, *Technics and Time 1: The Fault of Epimetheus*, trans. Richard Beardsworth and George Collins (Stanford: Stanford University Press, 1998). See also Ben Roberts, "Stiegler Reading Derrida: The Prosthesis of Deconstruction in Technics," *Postmodern Culture* 16.1 (September 2005), n.pag.

[26] Martin Heidegger, "The Question Concerning Technology," *Basic Writings, from "Being and Time" (1927) to "The Task of Thinking" (1964)*, ed. David Farrell Krell (London: Routledge and Kegan Paul, 1978) 294. For a larger context recaling ancient oppositions to *technē*, see Arthur Bradley, "*Deus ex machina*: Towards a Philsophy of Religion and Technology," *Comparative Critical Studies* 2.2 (2005), especially 273-4.

[27] Derrida, *Of Grammatology*, 167.

whose technicity can be apprehended from the outset of "Freud and the Scene of Writing," when Derrida motivates his reticence to use Freudian concepts as they "belong to the history of metaphysics, that is, to the system of logocentric repression which was organised in order to exclude or to lower [...] the body of the *written trace* as a didactic and *technical metaphor*."[28] Before reemphasising, in a concluding summary, that "the Freudian concept of trace must be radicalised and extracted from the metaphysics of presence which still retains it,"[29] a scene/stage [*scène*] in which Freud's language is *"caught up,"* Derrida elegantly "stages" the Freudian *performance* in a movement and with a choice of terms that, steeped in Freud's own writing practice, orchestrate the redemption of technicity and writing as tracing from (metaphorical) derivativeness to confer back on them an originary, quasi-natural violence—in "Marx and Sons" Derrida will polemically recall that all his own texts take into account "the performative dimension (not only of language in the narrow sense, but also of what I call the trace and writing)":[30]

> Thus Freud performs for us the scene of writing [*nous fait la scène de l'écriture*]. Like all those who write. And like all who know how to write, he let the scene duplicate, repeat, and betray itself within the scene [...].
>
> In following the advance of the metaphors of path, trace, breach, of the march treading down a track which was opened by effraction through neurone, light or wax, wood or resin, in order violently to inscribe itself in nature, matter, or matrix; and in following the untiring reference to a dry stilus and a writing without ink; and in following the inexhaustible inventiveness and dreamlike renewal of mechanical models—the metonymy perpetually at work on the same metaphor, obstinately substituting trace for trace and machine for machine—we have been wondering just what Freud was doing.[31]

For Stiegler in "Derrida and Technology: Fidelity at the Limits of Deconstruction and the Prosthesis of Faith," the thinking of the trace, *différance* and arche-writing as technological was already formed during Derrida's engagement with Husserl's *Origin of Geometry*.[32] The main thesis of this provocative essay is the dual

[28] Derrida, *Writing and Difference*, 248—emphases added.

[29] Derrida, *Writing and Difference*, 289.

[30] Jacques Derrida, "Marx & Sons," *Ghostly Demarcations: A Symposium on Jacques Derrida's "Specters of Marx,"* intro. Michael Sprinkler (London: Verso, 1999) 224.

[31] Derrida, *Writing and Difference*, 288.

[32] Bernard Stiegler, "Derrida and Technology: Fidelity at the Limits of Deconstruction and the Prosthesis of Faith," *Jacques Derrida and the Humanities: A Critical Reader*, ed. Tom Cohen (Cambridge: Cambridge University Press, 2001) 241.

articulation of deconstruction both as a thinking of fidelity[33] and as "a thinking of technics, of tele-technologies [...], of the "media" in all its guises—beginning with the most primal traces that launch the process of hominisation [...] and extending as far as the Web and all forms of technical archiving and high-fidelity [*sic*] recording, including those of the biotechnologies."[34] In the wake of Stiegler's *Technics and Time*, Arthur Bradley has suggested that this originary technicity is in Derrida "a static *logic* that exists outside time," and Richard Beardsworth that Derrida's deconstruction of the impossible aporia of logic *qua* the aporia of time leads to "an open set of "quasi-transcendental" logics which turn the relation between the human and the technical into a "logic" of supplementarity without history (the technical determinations of temporalisation)."[35] Against such reservations, I would claim that Derrida's originary technicity haunts as much as it is haunted by the productive work of the generalisable operation of *différance* as tempor(al)isation,[36] upon which the historicity of given technologies, even unthought, future teletechnologies,[37] must still be made to hinge, failing which the very necessity to historicise would (re-)form what *Glas* called a "transcendental contraband"—just as, according to Geoffrey Bennington, Stiegler's *Technics and Time* confuses the quasi-trascendental (originary technicity) and transcendental contraband (technics), and thus becomes a phenomenological anthropology of deconstruction:[38]

---

[33] Cf. especially Jacques Derrida's essay "Faith and Knowledge: The Two Sources of 'Religion' at the Limits of Reason Alone," trans. Samuel Weber, *Religion*, eds. Jacques Derrida and Gianni Vattimo (Cambridge: Polity, 1998) 1-78. I have discussed this strand of Derridean thought in "Believing in Deconstruction," forthcoming in the proceedings of the *Theory, Faith, Culture* conference (Cardiff University, 4-6 July 2007), ed. Chris Weedon.

[34] Stiegler, "Derrida and Technology: Fidelity at the Limits of Deconstruction and the Prosthesis of Faith," 239.

[35] See Arthur Bradley, "Originary Technicity: Technology and Anthropology," *Technicity*, eds. Arthur Bradley and Louis Armand (Prague: Litteraria Pragensia, 2006) 93; and Richard Beardsworth, *Derrida and the Political* (London and New York: Routledge, 1996) 154. Cf. also Beardsworth's "From a Genealogy of Matter to a Politics of Memory: Stiegler's Thinking of Technics," *Tekhnema: Journal of Philosophy and Technology* 2 (1995): 85-115.

[36] E.g. Derrida, "Différance," 8; 13; 15.

[37] Both Derrida and Stiegler have discussed these more contemporary teletechnologies in the series of exchanges *Echographies of Television: Filmed Interviews*, trans. Jennifer Bajorek (Cambridge: Polity, 2002).

[38] See Geoffrey Bennington, *Interrupting Derrida* (London: Routledge, 2000) 171, in the light of his earlier discussion of the contraband in *Glas*: "One can state as a law that any attempt to explain transcendental effects by invoking history must presuppose the historicity of that same history as the very transcendental which the system of explanation will never be able to comprehend. This [...] transcendental contraband [...] cannot resolve the paradox (*plus de ...*) according to which it is the very concept to which appeal is made to explain everything that will never be understood in the expla-

Can *différance*, for these reasons, settle down into the division of the ontico-ontological difference, such as it is thought, such as its "epoch" in particular is thought, "through," if it may still be expressed such, Heidegger's uncircumventable meditation? [cf. *Of Grammatology*, 23]
There is no simple answer to such a question.
In a certain aspect of itself, *différance* is certainly but the historical and epochal *unfolding* of Being or of the ontogical difference. The *a* of *différance* marks the *movement* of this unfolding.
And yet, are not the thought of the *meaning* or *truth* of Being, the determination of *différance* as the ontico-ontological difference, difference thought within the horizon of the question of *Being*, still intrametaphysical effects of *différance*? The unfolding of *différance* is perhaps not solely the truth of Being, or of the epochality of Being. Perhaps we must attempt to think this unheard-of thought, this silent tracing: that the history of Being, whose thought engages the Greco-Western *logos* such as it is produced via the ontological difference, is but an epoch of the *diapherein*. Henceforth one could no longer even call this an "epoch," the concept of epochality belonging to what is within history as the history of Being. Since Being has never had a "meaning," has never been thought or said as such, except by dissimulating itself in beings, then *différance*, in a certain and very strange way, (is) "older" than the ontological difference or than the truth of Being. When it has this age it can be called the play of the trace. The play of a trace which no longer belongs to the horizon of Being, but whose play transports and encloses the meaning of Being: the play of the trace, or the *différance*, which has no meaning and is not. Which does not belong.[39]

Such an attribution of temporal *ek-stasis* to deconstruction's originary technicity thus fails to take into account what I will tentatively call the "'epochality' of the *quasi*" that is breached/broached by the arche-trace as originary tempor(al)isation, without which no opening of "historical time" would have happened: "In the originary temporalisation and the movement of relationship with the outside, as Husserl actually describes them, non-presentation or depresentation is as "originary" as presentation. *That is why a thought of the trace can no more break with a transcendental phenomenology than be reduced to it.*"[40] And it is to one privileged aspect of this more originary phenomenological reduction known as "epochality,"

nation." (Geoffrey Bennington and Jacques Derrida, *Jacques Derrida*, trans. Geoffrey Bennington [Chicago and London: University of Chicago Press, 1993] 281-2).
[39] Derrida, *Margins of Philosophy*, 22.
[40] Derrida, *Of Grammatology*, 62.

related to "a suspensive withdrawal [*retrait*] of Being,"[41] that I now need to return, as promised.

4. The *retrait* of the trace

In a follow-up to his ground-breaking essay on philosophy's *usure* (i.e. wear and tear but also usura as surplus value) of metaphor in "White Mythology," while providing in the first part a patient refutation of Paul Ricoeur's subsequent objections in *La Métaphore vive* after a brilliant two-page-long performative *dérive* on various (not-so-) "metaphorical" means of transport (in modern Greek *metaphorikos* still denotes everything that pertains to transport), Derrida's "The Retrait of Metaphor" (1978) elaborates on the "structure of quasimetaphoricity" allegedly more originary than the distinction between metaphor and concept, and analyses it in terms of the Heideggerian notion of the trait (*Zug*) and its cognate derivatives: *Bezug* (rapport), *Entziehung* (*retrait*), etc. But as Gasché aptly comments, "the quasimetaphoricity of the trait through which a relation or reference in general is traced [...] also implies an originary withdrawal, a *retrait* or retreat of the trait." To which he further adds, implictly recalling the movement of the trace-as-effacement: "It is by the *retrait* of the trait that the originary tropic movements of metaphoricity permit the likes of the proper, the concept, Being [...] to come forth as the very obliteration of their relation to the trait."[42] Because the trait is "essentially" *retrait*, metaphoricity does not reveal itself as such and the act of grounding is a tracing marked by self-effacing. And since, for Heidegger, the problematic of the trait is linked to the question of Being, the trait of Being revealing itself in its very withdrawal, "in the same way as the trait of Being is at once the retreat (*retrait*) of Being, the mark that is folded upon itself, the re-marked trace, also retreats in its being."[43]

Picking up on his teasing opening gambit about the passing (itself) (away) of metaphor, Derrida notes in self-deconstructing syntactical fashion that the metaphor "se passe d'elle-même" at the moment of its *retrait* (its most pervsaive re-mark economically coinciding with its withdrawal), which would have the paradoxical form "of an overabundant remanence, of an intrusive repetition, always marking with a supplementary trait, with one more turn [*tour de plus*], with a re-turn and with a *re-trait* the trait that it will

---

41 Jacques Derrida, "The Retrait of Metaphor," trans. F. Gasdner, et al., *Enclitic* 2.2 (1978): 20. I have silently added elements from the French whenever necessary and systematically substituted *re(-)trait* for the translator's usual choice of "withdrawal."

42 Gasché, *The Tain of the Mirror*, 311.

43 Gasché, *The Tain of the Mirror*, 292.

have left right on the text."[44] This (sub/re)traction is also Heidegger's *retrait* of being indissociable from the movement of presence and truth-as-*aletheia*. The being of metaphor, this rapport (*Bezug*) which marks the *retrait* (*Entziehung*) of being, can only be apprehended "*quasi*-metaphorically, according to a metaphor of metaphor, with the surcharge of a supplementary trait, of a *retrait*,"[45] whose "*graphique*" (Derrida's own word) he then sketches out in terms echoing the earlier problematic of the trace, especially in "Freud and the Scene of Writing" (e.g. the Freudian, now Heideggerian *Bahnung* or *frayage*: breaching). Dissecting the rapport between metaphysics and metaphorics—onto which, to simplify brutally, he maps that of the retrait of being to the erasability of the trace—and especially the propriation, yet irreducible alterity, of *Denken* (thinking) and *Dichten* (composing, *poiein*) in Heidegger's "The Nature of Language" (1957), his thinking *and* his language (especially its "metaphorics"),[46] Derrida then emphasises two intersecting linguistic families: that of *Zug*, already mentioned, but also that of *Riss*,[47] especially *Aufriss*, often translated as *tracé-ouvrant* or *gravure* in French, and for which he substitutes his own *entame* (incision). Derrida then asks:

What then is the trait of this *Bezug* between *Denken* and *Dichten*? It is the trait of an incision (*entame*), of a tracing, *breaching* [cf. *Bahnen*] opening, of an *Aufriss*.

[The trait of the incision] withdraws [*se retire*], it is structurally in withdrawal, as a gap [*écart*—palindrome of *trace*], opening, differentiality, trace, border, traction, effraction, etc. From the moment that it withdraws in drawing itself out [*en se tirant*], the trait is *a priori* withdrawal, unappearance, and effacement of its mark in its incision [*entame*].
      Its inscription, as I have attempted to articulate it in the trace or in differance, *succeeds only in being effaced* [n'arrive qu'à s'effacer].
      It happens and comes about only in effacing itself. Inversely, the trait is not derived. [...] The *re-* of *retrait* is not an accident occurring to the trait.[48]

⁴⁴ Derrida, "The Retrait of Metaphor," 8—trans. modified.
⁴⁵ Derrida, "The Retrait of Metaphor," 21—trans. modified.
⁴⁶ Soon after recalling "the trait or the differential traction as a possibility of language [*langage*], of *logos*, of the language [*langue*] and of *lexis* in general, of spoken inscription just as much as written" (Derrida, "The Retrait of Metaphor," 27).
⁴⁷ Still in the footsteps of Heidegger, Derrida will return to the problematic of the trait and the *retrait*, their *frayage* (path-breaking), via the *Riss* and *Zug* families in the self-division and relation of spirit to itself in *Of Spirit: Heidegger and the Question*, trans. Geoffrey Bennington and Rachel Bowlby (Chicago and London: University of Chicago Press, 1989) especially 104-7.
⁴⁸ Derrida, "The Retrait of Metaphor," 28-29.

Like the trace, therefore, the trait's originary condition and/as destining ("*arrive*") lies in its self-effacing as always already a re-mark, a re-trace, a re(-)trait.

Cutting through many layers and folds, I hasten onto Derrida's third and final conclusive "remark":

> We have just glimpsed the trait contracting with itself, withdrawing, crossing and intersecting [*recoupant*] itself across these two neighboring circumscriptions of *Reissen* and *Ziehen*. [...] In the intersection [*recoupe*], the trait is itself remarked while withdrawing, it succeeds in effacing itself [*arrive à s'effacer*] in an other [...]. The trait is retrait. We can no longer even say *is*, we can no longer submit the retrait to the instance of an ontological copula [...]: the trait treats or is treated, traces the trait, therefore retraces and re-treats [*re-traite*] or withdraws [*retire*] the retrait, contracts, is contracted and signs with itself, with the retrait of itself, a strange contract [...]. We must again, right here, perform, incise, trace, tract, track [...] the capture [...] of this crossing aligning *Reissen* and *Ziehen* [...].[49]

Tracing but also tracting and tracking, thus joining technicity and animality under the auspices of a "*suis*" (am/follow):

> The retrait [...] *withdraws* itself [*se* retire] both from the Being of being [*de l'être de l'étant*] as such and from language [...]. It withdraws *itself* [se *retire*] but the ipseity of the *se* (itself) by which it would be related to itself with a trait or line does not precede it and already supposes a supplementary trait in order to be traced [*se tracer*], signed, withdrawn [*retirer*], retraced in its turn. *Retraits* thus writes itself in the plural [...], divides itself and reassembles in the retrait of the retrait. It is what I have elsewhere tried to name *pas* as well. It is a question here of the path again, of what passes there, of what passes it by, happens there, or not [*de ce qui y passe, le passe, s'y passe, ou pas*].
>
> What is happening? [*Qu'est-ce qui se passe*] will I have asked in opening [*entamant*] this discourse? Nothing, no response, if not that the retrait of/from metaphor happens and with(out) itself [*se passe et de lui-même*].[50]

"The trait is therefore nothing,"[51] just as it is said in *Of Grammatology* that "[t]he trace is nothing, it is not an entity, it exceeds the question *What is?*" or, later on: "*The trace itself does not exist*,"[52] two statements which uncannily chime with Derrida's double quip towards the close of "Letter to a Japanese Friend" — "What decon-

49 Derrida, "The Retrait of Metaphor," 31 — trans. modified.
50 Derrida, "The Retrait of Metaphor," 33 — trans. modified.
51 Derrida, "The Retrait of Metaphor," 32.
52 Derrida, *Of Grammatology*, 75; 167.

struction is not? everything of course! / What is deconstruction? nothing of course!"[53] — but which I will later take up in a final movement against the background—or is it the figure?—of the anagrammatic relation between the "archaic" French verb for being, *ester*, its *retrait* in *rester* (from *re-stare*), and the "almost nothing" of cinders.

5. From arche-writing to archival impression

Still hot on the track or trail of the Derridean trace, we now arrive at *Archive Fever*, Derrida's meditation on the complex imbrications of remembrance and (especially new) teletechnologies in the archive, which marks his return to Freud's concern with mnemonics and techniques of inscription (its subtitle is "A Freudian Impression"). At least two passages from "Freud and the Scene of Writing," their recall in "Différance," and one from *Of Grammatology* had envisaged the space of impression or (mnemonic) inscription as dependent on the trace as erasure, capitalising on the earlier work on Husserl, in ways that could be said to anticipate some of the concerns about the archive in a more modern technological world, some twenty-five years later:

> The path is broken, cracked, *fracta*, breached. Now there would be two kinds of neurones: the permeable neurones (φ), which offer no resistance and thus retain no trace of impression, would be the perceptual neurones [...].[54]

> Traces thus produce the space of their inscription only by acceding to the period of their erasure. From the beginning, in the "present" of their first impression, they are constituted by the double force of repetition and erasure, legibility and illegibility.[55]

> The two apparently different values of *différance* are tied together in Freudian theory: to differ as discernibility, distinction, separation, diastem, *spacing*; and to defer as detour, relay, reserve, temporisation.
> 1. The concepts of trace (*Spur*), of breaching (*Bahnung*), and of the forces of breaching [...] are inseparable from the concept of difference. The origin of memory, and of the psyche as (conscious or unconscious) memory in general, can be described only by taking into account the difference between breaches. Freud says so

[53] Jacques Derrida, "Letter to a Japanese Friend," trans. David Wood and Andrew Benjamin, *A Derrida Reader: Between the Blinds*, ed. Peggy Kamuf (New York: Harvester Wheatsheaf, 1991) 275.
[54] Derrida, *Writing and Difference*, 252.
[55] Derrida, *Writing and Difference*, 284.

overtly. There is no breach without difference and no difference without trace.

2. All the differences in the production of unconscious traces and in the processes of inscription (*Niederschrift*) can also be interpreted as moments of *différance*, in the sense of putting into reserve.[56]

Even before it is linked to incision, engraving, drawing, or the letter [...], the concept of the *graphie* implies the framework of the *instituted trace*, as the possibility common to all systems of signification.[57]

And quite explicitly, Derrida called *différance*, or the (arche-)trace, the "being-imprinted of the imprint" (*être imprimé de l'empreinte*).[58]

Within an interpretive framework restating the distinctions, briefly sketched in the earlier essay from *Writing and Difference*,[59] between various types of mnemonic inscription inherited from the Platonic opposition between *mnēmē* ("live," conscious memory) or *anamnēsis* (the Socratic recollection of the immortal soul) and *hypomnēma* (the artificial or technical supplement to memory),[60] *Archive Fever* puts forward hypotheses which share a common "trait" as "[t]hey all concern the *impression* left [...] by the *Freudian signature* on its own archive, on the concept of the archive and of archivisation" as those are indissociable from "*a place of consignation*" and "*a technique of repetition*."[61] (As an aside, one would need to elaborate at much greater length the role of Derrida's conception of memory as active breaching (Freud's *Bahnung*) here, for instance in the light of the following passages from *Writing and Difference*: "Memory, thus, is not a psychical property among others; it is the *very* essence of the psyche: resistance, and precisely, thereby, an opening to the effraction of the trace," and: "Trace as memory is not a pure breaching that might be reappropriated at any time as simple presence; it is rather the ungraspable and invisible difference between breaches."[62])

Profoundly at work within the (constitution/institution of) the archive is an "anarchivic" or "archiviolithic" (i.e. archive-destroying) drive which "works *to destroy the archive: on the condition of ef-*

---

56 Derrida, *Margins of Philosophy*, 18 ("Différance").

57 Derrida, *Of Grammatology*, 46.

58 Derrida, *Of Grammatology*, 63.

59 Derrida, "Structure, Sign and Play in the Discourse of the Human Sciences," 278-9; 286.

60 Jacques Derrida, *Archive Fever: A Freudian Impression*, trans. Eric Prenowitz (Chicago and London: University of Chicago Press, 1995) 11ff. See also the fuller discussion of *hypomnesis* in "Plato's Pharmacy," *Dissemination*, trans. Barbara Johnson (London: Athlone, 1981) 61-171.

61 Derrida, *Archive Fever*, 5; 11.

62 Derrida, "Freud and the Scene of Writing," 252; 253.

facing but also *with a view to effacing* its own "proper" traces."[63] This destructive death drive

> not only incites [...] amnesia, the annihilation of memory, as *mnēmē* or *anamnēsis*, but also commands [cf. what *arkhē* also means: commencement as much as commandment] the radical effacement, in truth the eradication, of that which can never be reduced to *mnēmē* or to *anamnēsis*, that is, the archive, consignation, the documentary or monumental apparatus as *hypomnēma*, mnemotechnical supplement or representative, auxiliary or memo-randum.[64]

Thus archiving means *a priori* erasing and destroying.

Derrida then returns to Freud's "mystic pad" (*Wunderblock*), "the technical model of the machine tool, intended [...] to *represent on the outside* memory as *internal* archivisation,"[65] and, after quoting extensively from his earlier essay,[66] wonders whether "the structure of the psychic apparatus, this system, at once mnesic and hypomnesic, which Freud sought to describe within the "mystic pad," resist the evolution of archival techno-science or not."[67] He will revisit this issue in the "Preamble," asking himself "what is the moment *proper* to the archive" as "a certain hypomnesic and prosthetic experience of the technical substrate,"[68] and distinguishing between three meanings of "impression":

a) scriptural or typographical (*Niederschrift*), of the press, of printing, of the imprint, which he had privileged in his former texts;

b) as idea not fully concpetualised, of the system of mnemic in-scription according to Freud, including such "techniques" of the psychical apparatus as repression (*Verdrängung*) and suppression (*Verdrückung*) — cf. page 81, note: "prosthesis of repression";

c) as signature and countersignature, extending the reflection on the impact or *legs* (legacy) of the Freud family on the institution of psychoanalysis already undertaken in "Speculate — On Freud."

In the near-final "Theses," the tension between the originary, yet lost "live" memory and its subsequent *re*collection, and the technical substratum necessary for archivisation, is given one more thought:

> Freud made possible the idea of an archive properly speaking, of a hypomnesic or technical archive, of the substrate or the subjectile

[63] Derrida, *Archive Fever*, 10.
[64] Derrida, *Archive Fever*, 11; for definition of *arkhē* see pages 1-2.
[65] Derrida, *Archive Fever*, 13.
[66] Cf. *Writing and Difference*, 227-8.
[67] Derrida, *Archive Fever*, 15.
[68] Derrida, *Archive Fever*, 25.

(material or virtual) which, in what is already a psychic *spacing*, cannot be reduced to memory: neither to memory as conscious reserve [i.e. *mnēmē*], nor to memory as rememoration, as an act of recalling [i.e. *anamnēsis*] [...]. But [...] this does not stop Freud [...] from holding the technical prosthesis to be a secondary and accessory exteriority. In spite of resorting to what he holds to be a model of auxiliary representation, he invariably maintains a primacy of live memory and anamnesis in their originary tenporalisation.[69]

The word "subjectile," used on several occasions throughout *Archive Fever*, echoes the title of a 1986 essay on Antonin Artaud's idiosyncratic writing practices, in which Derrida had put forward this nonce word to designate the technical support or substrate necessary for the subject to be grounded, the prosthetic machinic extension of the human in writing.[70] It partly "translates" and rewrites both the Greek *hypomnēma*, the "mnemotechnical supplement or representative" "which can never be reduced to *mnēmē* or to *anamnēsis*," in prey to "radical effacement" (cf. above), and *hypokheimenon*, the "substance" (literally: under-lying, under-thrown) as support for an essence, from which the "subject" was derived. Within a reflection on the archive and archvisation, and an implicit redeployment of the trace as inscription/impression, the subjectile is the support of the trace which points to the materialisation of the "originary temporalisation" or supplementary *spacing* of being (*être*) as *restance*.

6. Reste—the zoontotechnic "nature" of the trace
Whereas Derrida's installation of technicity at the heart of the nonhuman trace had been taken to task for its timid thinking of the technic as such, or its residual ideality in breaking down the divide between thinking (philosophy) and technology, Arthur Bradley conversely asks about Stiegler's own approach: "To what extent is Stiegler's definition of the human as constituted by technics also bought at the expense of depriving it of an independent ontic status?"[71] Rather than addressing the objection this time, I would like to take it as my cue to highlight—provocatively for a thinker known primarily for his deconstruction of ontology—how the technicity of the Derridean arche-trace arguably eschews such a reservation.

---

[69] Derrida, *Archive Fever*, 91-92.
[70] It was first translated as "Maddening the Subjectile," trans. Mary Ann Caws, *Yale French Studies* 84: "Boundaries: Writing and Drawing" (1994): 154-71.
[71] Arthur Bradley, "Originary Technicity: Technology and Anthropology," 85.

It will be remembered that Heidegger proposed to inquire into the nontechnological essence of technology and how it relates to the unconcealment of *aletheia*, warning as to the "danger" (*Gefahr*; cf. Heidegger's *Bahnung*, or *frayage*, and his opening that we should pay heed to the "way") of its attempt to enclose all beings in a given claim (ordering man and nature towards the aim of total mastery), an "enframing" he calls *Ge-stell* which, as the essence of technology, would reduce man to a "standing reserve," or *Bestand*.[72] (It is perhaps also with this Heideggerian note in mind that one should hear Derrida's echo of his now canonical description of writing in *Of Grammatology*, applied in "The Rhetoric of Drugs" to technology as a "dangerous supplement" "'originarily' at work and in place in the supposedly ideal interiority of the 'body and soul.'"[73])

Commenting on how Heidegger—for whom modern technology is a challenging "which puts to nature the unreasonable demand that it supply energy which can be extracted and stored as such"[74]—draws together the families of words derived from *stehen* and *stellen*, operating a transformation of *Bestellen* as producing, establishing, in-stalling, into essentially a *Stellen* as provoking, extracting,[75] Lacoue-Labarthe glosses as follows in "Typography":

> Perhaps this mutation is to be thought of as the passage from the pure and simple *stal* [*étal*] or *display* [*étalement*]—which, after all, would render fairly well one of the senses of *logos* privileged by Heidegger—to all the modern forms of *installation* or *establishment*, from the State (its *constitution* and its *institutions*)[76] up to the generalised *show* (*étalage*) of the market economy. Changed into "provoking installation," *poiesis* would become the unrestrained pursuit of that which has always sustained it and which it perhaps no longer has (of which it perhaps no longer *disposes*), namely of a being "set upright," of the *stable* and the *static* (*Stand, station*), of the place in which to stand up (*Stelle*), and posture or position (*Stellung*), which it identifies with the "standing reserve" (with consistency or with the *store, Bestand*) by which the mode of pres-

---

[72] Heidegger, "The Question Concerning Technology," 298; 301-2. See also the Addendum to "The Origin of the Work of Art," *Poetry, Language, Thought*, trans. Albert Hofstadter (New York: Harper and Row, 1971) 82-84.

[73] Jacques Derrida, *Points... Interviews 1974-1994*, ed. Elizabeth Weber, trans. Peggy Kamuf (Stanford: Stanford University Press, 1995) 244-5.

[74] Heidegger, "The Question Concerning Technology," 296.

[75] cf. "The Question Concerning Technology," 302.

[76] On a tangential note, it is interesting to compare this development with Beardsworth's ingenious formulation that, for Derrida, arche-writing "is an *originary structure of repetition*, constitutes the structure of the "instituted trace" which comprehends the foundation, exclusion and contradiction of (the history of) linguistics." See Richard Beardsworth, *Derrida and the Political* (London and New York: Routledge, 1996) 17 (12-18 for the sub-section on "The Instituted Trace and Arche-Writing").

ence of the present is determined in the modern age—the present itself being thought, for this reason, as object (*Gegenstand*) according to the dominating orientation of the metaphysics of subjectivity.[77]

Thus, from Heidegger's critique of the oblivion by metaphysics of the early trace of Being as well as of the essence of technology, one can still exhume the distorted remains of some form of Hegelian *Aufhebung* or *relève* in his lexical gathering[78] or "orthodramatisation"[79] of subjectivity and essence in language, unlike the whole "desistential" adventure of deconstruction,[80] notably *Glas*, "fall-erected" as a tombstone on the remains of Hegel's Absolute Knowledge. Thus "L'animal que [...] je suis [...] relève des traces," on page 83 of *L'Animal que donc je suis*, must also be heard against the Hegelian *Aufhebung* or *relève*, which negates as it sublates, and to which Derrida counterpoints operations like the reserve and the *garde* within the erasable trace of *différance*. The deconstructive syntax here "translates" the synthetic reduction and subjugation afforded by Hegelian sublation (*Aufhebung*), to which the animal has been subjected throughout the history of metaphysics (*relever de*: to depend on, to come under the jurisdiction of), into the possibility of the animal's self-conscious interaction with its own traces, including by erasing them (*relever des empreintes*— imprints; cf. "impression"—to take finger- or footprints): *capio ergo sum*.[81] And the "*Je le suis à la trace*," brought up earlier, can now also be understood as the coupling of the ontic and the technic in the zoic, thus blazing a trail, via the trace, beyond the non-technological understanding of the essence of technology in Heidegger's "The Question Concerning Technology."

[77] Philippe Lacoue-Labarthe, *Typography: Mimesis, Philosophy, Politics*, intro. Jacques Derrida, ed. Christopher Fynsk (Cambridge, Mass: Harvard University Press, 1989) 67. See also 66-67 notes 31 and 33.

[78] I am referring here to Heidegger's frequent etymological gloss of *logos* as "gathering," from *legein*, especially in "The Anaximander Fragment" and "Logos."

[79] Used by Lacan towards the end of "Presentation on Transference" to recall that the psychoanalyst's role was "that of a positive nonaction aiming at the orthodramatisatiomn of the patient's subjectivity"; Jacques Lacan, *Écrits*, trans. Bruce Fink, in collaboration with Héloïse Fink and Russell Grigg (New York and London: Norton, 2006) 184.

[80] Cf. Jacques Derrida's introduction to the Lacoue-Labarthe volume, "Desistance," especially the section on "*Ge-stell*" (*Typography*, 15-25). See also René Major, *Lacan avec Derrida. Analyse désistentielle* (Paris: Mentha, 1991), and "Reason from the Unconscious," trans. Geoffrey Bennington and Rachel Bowlby, *Oxford Literary Review* 12.1-2: "Psychoanalysis and Literature; New York," eds. Nicholas Royle and Ann Wordsworth (1990), especially 24-25, about the *désistance* of Being and truth, "its disinstallation and its unsealing in a de-steling [*déstèlement*]."

[81] Cf. Derrida, "The Animal That Therefore I Am (More to Follow)," 417-8.

Against the Heideggerian re-tracing and "erection" of the essence of technology remains Derrida's *restance* of the arche-trace which *n'arrive qu'à s'effacer* and whose disseminal remainders include especially cinders, as in the five obsessional words that stalk through several of his texts, from *Dissemination* onwards and via *The Post Card*, until they culminate in a more sustained poetic meditation in *Feu la cendre* (*Cinders*): "*il y a là cendre.*"[82] Substituting a Mallarméan "pure place" as well as the poet's famous "nothing will have taken place but the place"[83] for essential determination, Derrida's haunting, talismanic leitmotif timidly proclaims the mystery of a self-effacing, inessential trace which "remains without remaining": "the incinerated is no longer nothing, nothing but the cinder, [...] a remnant [*reste*] that must no longer remain."[84] And, says one of two voices in this poetic meditation, which I will counterpoint with an excerpt from the contemporaneous essay "How To Avoid Speaking: Denegations":

> I have the impression now that the best paradigm for the trace, for him, is not, as some have believed, and he as well, perhaps, the trail of the hunt, the fraying [*frayage*—i.e. *Bahnung*, Freudian or Heideggerian], the furrow in the sand, the wake in the sea, the love of the step for its imprint, but the cinder [...][85]

> Une trace a eu lieu. [...] même si elle *n'arrive qu'à s'effacer*, si elle n'advient qu'en effaçant, l'effacement aura eu lieu, fût-il de cendre. Il y a là cendre.[86]

The trace as spacing, which removes *the* place from (the) taking place, is what, in *Echographies of Television*, Derrida will recall has always been what "deconstruction" endeavoured to articulate:

> I say "deconstruction" because, ultimately, what I name and try to think under this word is, at bottom, nothing other than this very process ["the accelerated development of teletechnologies, of cyberspace, of the new topology of the 'virtual'"], its "taking place" in such a way that its happening affects the very experience of place, and the recording [...] of this "thing," the trace that traces (inscribes, preserves, carries, refers, or defers) the différance of this

---

[82] This long-standing obsession is itself evoked towards the beginning of *Cinders / Feu la cendre*, trans. Ned Lukacher (Lincoln and London: University of Nebraska Press, 1991) 21.

[83] Derrida, *Cinders*, especially 37.

[84] Derrida, *Cinders*, 37.

[85] Derrida, *Cinders*, 43.

[86] Jacques Derrida, "Comment ne pas parler: Dénégations" (1986), *Psyché. Inventions de l'autre* (Paris: Galilée, 1987) 560-1; compare with the attempt at an English translation in "How to Avoid Speaking: Denials," trans. Ken Frieden, *Derrida and Negative Theology*, eds. Harold Coward and Toby Foshay (Albany: SUNY Press, 1992) 98.

event which happens to place [*qui arrive au lieu*]—which happens to take place, and to taking-place [*qui arrive à (l')avoir-lieu*].[87]

Reste, from *re-stare*, *retrait* of *stare* as *être* or, archaically, *ester*, desisting from Heidegger's essential "orthodramatisation" of Being as *stare* in the Germanic family of *stehen* (passive) and *stellen* (active), from which the German philosopher uncovered and rethought the dangerous essence of technology: such is "in the end" too [*n'arrive qu'à*] Derrida's more modest, subdued (arche-)trace, the almost nothing of the event (taking place) called "deconstruction."

---

[87]   Derrida, *Echographies of Television*, 36.

Louis Armand

Grammatica Speculativa

> The interoperable network ... represents the decisive element in the globalisation of the technical system. Through it, mnemotechnology effectively becomes the centrepiece of this system.
>
> —Bernard Stiegler, *La technique et le temps: le temps du cinéma*

Within the discourse of post-humanism there will always have been an alibi for the détournement of scientific epistemologies towards political "ends." Yet the interface of the human and the machine, and the prosthetic reinvention of "man," cannot simply be *reduced* to an ideological event: wherever scientific discourse approaches the limits of what is calculable or definable, the political accedes to a material reality that is no longer subject to conventional discourses of knowledge, control or verification. The insufficient scientific object becomes the political object par excellence, at precisely that point at which the fabric of the real meshes with what we might call an apparatus of the unthought: an apparatus which is nevertheless programmemable, is indeed the programmeme itself. It is the point at which command determines not the actions we attribute to the real, but its conditions. For this reason, it is not a question of rendering or affecting material behaviour in opposition to the so-called laws of nature, but of situating the discursive conditions of such behaviour, not as *re*-programmemed but as "originarily" programmematic. Such is the character of the problem that has in recent discussion accompanied the logic of interactivity—whether it define a relation between two subjects or between the organic and the inorganic, nature and machine, human and computer—wherein the definitional character of intelligence and the demystifications of mind-control brought about by modern neuroscience have set new stakes in the contest of reason and the unthought.

1. In the introductory chapter of his study of media art, entitled *Interzone*, Darren Tofts writes: "If the last decade of the 20th-century is to be remembered by one word, it would have to be 'interactive.'"[1] The term "interactive" here refers to a particular interface phenomenon that is as old as the human story itself — which is to say, as old as language — but that obtains its particular contemporary inflection with the advent of the electronic digital computer and of global communication systems. John Dewey, for whom the experiential dimension of language defines the basic criteria for any conception of man, has suggested that "we can recognise that all human conduct is *interaction* between elements of human nature and the environment, natural and social."[2] And in this context, the human-computer interaction can perhaps be considered simply one more step in the evolution of a semantically contoured mind-ecology, from animism to post-industrialism, illustrating a particular idea of progress in the inventions of automata and automatism — or what Henri Lefebvre terms "cybernated human robots"[3] — by which certain aspects of the material world manifest an *active* subjection to man's will. Indeed, interactivity has always presupposed some form of material "entity" capable of receiving and processing commands — whether these be primitive mnemotechnical systems, magic formulae, machine code or computing programmematics — and in doing so manifesting, not simply a prosthetic extension, but rather something like a mimēsis or mirror-effect of linguistic agency. In each case, interactivity presupposes a condition in which the otherwise inert, mechanical or technological, replies to the idea of man.

The identification of interactivity as a phenomenon particular to the end of the 20th-century is linked to the radical transformation of daily life that followed the integration of computing into all spheres of human activity; no longer as the event-horizon of science fiction scenarios or dreams of immersive virtual reality (as in William Gibson's *matrix*), but as the very "medium" of quotidian experience. Such a transformation had long been anticipated by Marshall McLuhan and others, who situated the "medium" of the digital age not in specific technological artefacts, but precisely in the technics of interactivity as a general, structural condition of "consciousness"[4] — one vested in the relational character of language, of

---

[1] Darren Tofts, *Interzone* (Sydney: Craftsman House, 2005) 7.
[2] John Dewey, *Human Nature and Conduct* (New York: Henry Holt, 1922) 10.
[3] Henri Lefebvre, *Introduction to Modernity*, trans. John Moore (London: Verso, 1995) 254.
[4] Marshall McLuhan, *Understanding Media: The Extensions of Man* (New York: McGraw-Hill, 1964).

"communication" broadly conceived, and of the very possibility of signification as such.

The computer age, as Tofts reminds us, "brought with it many promises, from speed and efficiency to the street directory for the global village. It connected us to the world in new and unforeseen ways, integrating people into networks, virtual communities that were every bit as real as our families and the people next door. With the computer network, interaction, once the province of face-to-face communications, extended its reach across impossible distances."[5] This brings into view another aspect of interactivity, which has to do with assumptions of locality and what might otherwise be called inter-subjectivity: the assumption, at least since Plato, that communication as inter-subjective experience presupposes presence. This presupposition has in itself been the object of extensive critique and when today we speak of such concepts as "telepresence" we are not, in fact, referring to some ontological excentricity, but rather to a constitutive condition of "presence" and "the present"—one which already in the Platonistic conception reveals itself to be technological.[6] The concept of presence has, indeed, always involved a certain distanciation and a certain technē: what we might regard as a signification-effect whose structure is always that of a "communication-at-a-distance," even when this supposed communication refers to a phenomenon of reflexivity. In other words, presence, even a presence-to-itself, remains tele-medial. And it is this qualified medial aspect that is most ubiquitously "evident" (even, or especially, through its increasingly invisible integration) in the advent of computer-based virtual environments and digital media.

2. The specific advent of what we now call "hypermedia"—a term coined in 1965 by Ted Nelson—was clearly prefigured in the emerging structuralist discourses of psychoanalysis, anthropology and semiotics, but particularly in the field of cybernetics and artificial intelligence. The basic tenets of cybernetics—initially framed by André-Marie Ampère in the 1840s as designating a science of "government"—are traceable to 17th and 18th-century preoccupations with systematisation and mechanistics, particularly to the rationalism of Newton and Descartes, and to a certain degree modern computing can be seen as a permutation of these existing ideas via 19th-century discourses on "ecology" (a term coined in 1866 by

---

[5] Tofts, *Interzone*, 7.
[6] Cf. Jacques Derrida and Bernard Stiegler, *Echographies of Television*, trans. Jennifer Bajorek (Cambridge: Polity, 2002).

Ernst Haeckel). Alan Turing, one of the architects of the electronic digital computer, had drawn attention in the 1950s to the fact that the basic approaches to programmeming machines developed during and immediately after WWII had already been elaborated in the work of Charles Babbage in the 1830s and '40s. Babbage's design for the "Analytical Engine" (foreshadowed in Denis Diderot's 1751 "stocking machine" and the Jacquard loom) included, among other things, "instruction tables," a memory "store," a calculating and decision-making "mill," augmented by techniques for programmeming which persist in more recent vernacular as "looping" and "branching."

Most significantly, Babbage's Analytical Engine was capable, at least hypothetically, of altering (within limits) its own stored programmeme—in other words of functioning recursively—thus complexifying the assumptions of a straightforwardly "logical" machine in which programmemed input is mechanically converted into an automatic output; a process that operates on the threshold, as Peirce suggested in 1887, of symbolic and semiotic re-production.[7] The crucial refinement to Babbage's hypothesis came with the practical application of electro-mechanisation and techniques of "autopoiesis" in the realisation of modern computing in the late 1940s. Previously it had been asserted by Babbage's assistant, Ada Byron (Countess Lovelace), that machines could only ever do what they were programmemed to do—an assertion which relies on the notion of a fully determinate science of logical complexity. "The Analytic Engine," Byron argued, "has no pretensions whatever to *originate* anything. It can do whatever we *know how to order it* to perform.[8] In Peirce's words, "every machine [...] is destitute of all originality."[9] Indeed, the taboo against self-producing, propagating or learning machines may be taken as a key distinction between earlier approaches to recursion and automation, and more recent cybernetic and state-based quantum-mechanical approaches—in which complexity is characterised not as an object-

[7] C.S. Peirce, "Logical Machines," *American Journal of Psychology* 1.1 (1887): 165-70.
[8] Cited in Douglas R. Hofstadter, *Gödel, Escher, Bach: An Eternal Golden Braid* (New York: Vintage Books, 1980) 25. Cf. Lady A.A. Lovelace (Byron), "Notes upon the Memoir, 'Sketch of the Analytical Engine Invented by Charles Babbage,' by L.F. Menabrea (Geneva, 1842)," *Charles Babbage and his Calculating Engines*, eds. P. and E. Morrison (New York: Dover, 1961) 284.
[9] Peirce, "Logical Machines," 168. Peirce refers to Jonathan Swift's satirical random text machine in book III of *Gulliver's Travels* (1726), by means of which "the most ignorant person, at a reasonable charge, and with a little bodily labour, might write books in philosophy, poetry, politics, laws, mathematics and theology, without he least assistance from genius or study" (165). See also Jonathan Swift, "A Discourse Concerning the Mechanical Operation of the Spirit," *A Tale of a Tub and Other Satires* (London: J.M. Dent, 1963) 169-187.

determined phenomenon but a systemic one (i.e. mechanical "state" and autopoietic "event" are seen as causally entangled).

One particular measure of this distinction can be found in two basic principles elaborated by Turing in his seminal 1936 paper on "Computable Numbers" and his 1950 paper on "Computing Machinery and Intelligence."[10] The first of these papers sets out to define computability in terms of the problem of "decidability" (vis-à-vis Hilbert's Entscheidungsproblem), proposing for this purpose an imaginary digital machine which would function as an "analogue" to a human computer (it is important to note here the computational function of the *human-analogue*: the "special property of digital computers" being their capacity to "mimic *any* discrete state machine," hence its *universal* characteristic, and hence also its value as a test of a generalised concept of "intelligence," as we shall see).

In effect, Turing's machine was a literate machine: it was supposed to be capable of reading (scanning) and inscribing marks, as well as following commands and modifying these commands as it proceeded, thereby modifying its own "behaviour." Since these commands were substantively identical to the marks the machine was supposed to read, erase and/or inscribe, Turing in effect reinvented the principle of machine programmeming as computer software: a type of "machine," as Jacques Lacan has said, made entirely of "words."[11] In his second paper, Turing pursued the obvious consequences of such a literate, self-modifying or self-programmeming "machine"—a machine, that is, possessing all the formal attributes of agency—towards a functional definition of intelligence. What is most notable about Turing's second paper, however, is that it situates intelligence not in terms of a phenomenon of consciousness, for example, or upon the basis of a claim that machines may "think" (such formulations are considered meaningless by Turing), but rather upon a particular effect of interactivity. Or, to be rather more precise, upon the illusion of an inter-*subjectivity*.

3. The interactivity-effect is delineated by Turing by means of what he calls the "imitation game" (or what is now referred to as the

---

[10] Alan Turing, "On Computable Numbers, with an Application to the Entscheidungsproblem," *Proceedings of the London Mathematical Society* 2.42 (1936): 230-265; "Computing Machinery and Intelligence," *Mind* LIX.236 (1950): 433-460.

[11] Jacques Lacan, "A Materialist Definition of the Phenomenon of Consciousness," *The Seminar of Jacques Lacan. Book II: The Ego in Freud's Theory and in the Technique of Psychoanalysis 1954-1955*, trans. S. Tomaselli (London: Cambridge University Press, 1988) 47

Turing Test), and it devolves upon the problem of whether or not a digital computer may be mistaken for a human being on the basis of a controlled scenario of questions and answers. This, as Turing recognised, is the old game of *viva voce* or dialectic, but played out by means of *written* messages between a human interrogator and two unseen "subjects": one human, one machine, which the interrogator is supposed to distinguish or identify correctly on the basis of their responses. The structure of the game may be described as sophistic, since the objective is ultimately to test the assumed truth-structures of discourse and the logic of verifiability. It is also designed to test the mimetic character of assumptions governing the ways in which we define such things as "intelligence." That is to say, how man seeks to find himself or his expectations in some way mirrored in what he sees or thinks he sees.

In this way, Turing's scenario exploits the "pathetic" or "affective" characteristic of so-called inter-subjective experience or communication, allowing the interrogator to imagine an interlocutor whose intelligence reflects his own—or in other words, reflects the "interpretive scene." (It is quite unnecessary, as Turing remarks, "to make a 'thinking machine' more human by dressing it up in [...] artificial flesh." A mirror, indeed a metaphor, is more than enough.)[12] The workings of this "pathetic fallacy," to borrow Ruskin's term,[13] are such as to emphasise both the humanistic basis of intelligence (which is thus viewed as essential rather than definitional) and the supposedly human character of any symbolic *medialisation* of experience. One of the consequences of Turing's test, however, is not only to expose certain flaws in the humanistic or essentialist view of intelligence, but to reveal the dogmatic underpinnings of the very notion of intelligence and consequently a certain blindness to the "exceptional" nature of those symbolic systems assumed to be the sole domain of man. Contrary to such assumptions, for any such system to be possible, a *general* condition of symbolisation must be assumed to exist somehow in what is called nature, and which would thus make available not only the "human exception," but also—and necessarily—what are called "animal languages" and "artificial intelligence."

---

[12] Turing, "Computing Machinery and Intelligence," 434.
[13] John Ruskin, "Of the Pathetic Fallacy," *Modern Painters* (New York: Knopf, 1988 [1856]) III.§5: "It will appear also, on consideration of the matter, that this fallacy is of two principal kinds. Either ... it is the fallacy of wilful fancy, which involves no real expectation that it will be believed; or else it is a fallacy caused by an excited state of the feelings, making us, for the time, more or less irrational ... The state of mind which attributes to it these characters of a living creature is one in which the reason is unhinged by grief. All violent feelings have the same effect. They produce in us a falseness in all our impressions of external things, which I would generally characterize as the 'Pathetic Fallacy.'"

This argument was already in part anticipated in the work of thinkers like Hippolyte Taine, according to whom—in Ernst Cassirer's paraphrase—"what we call 'intelligent behaviour' is not a special principle of human nature; it is only a more refined and complicated play of the same associative mechanisms and automatism which we find in all animal relations." Consequently: "If we accept this explanation the difference between intelligence and instinct becomes negligible; it is a mere difference of degree, not of quality. Intelligence itself becomes a useless and scientifically meaningless term."[14] Having taken this first step towards qualifying the human exception, it comes to appear that even the basic progressivist tenets of refinement and complexity cease to remain universally coherent. Moreover, instinct too—as we see in Freud—becomes a meaningless term which comes to be replaced increasingly by a notion of "unconscious" reflexivity, founded upon the tendency of all dynamic systems to be characterised by iterability, recursion and emergent structuration. Such features come not to be regarded as additions to material pre-conditions, but as conditions themselves, such that symbolic language, for example, ceases to appear as a strictly human domain and instead reveals itself to be bound up in a general mechanics that is as far from either progressivism or instinctualism as it is from a humanist metaphysics.

It is thus not simply metaphorical to suggest that the Turing Test defers the question of general intelligence onto the proposition of a discursive, "symbolic" machine—a machine made entirely out of signifiers, codes, "information"—capable of functioning as an analogue of the literate technology known as man, in whom (in turn) such things as the *action of judgement* are seen to mirror the mechanical "decision-making" enacted by the primitive *universal* Turing machine. The implications here for an understanding of human subjectivity, consciousness, agency, and rational thought become the subject of a series of seminars by Lacan during the mid-1950s, which re-examine—within a broadly cybernetic framework—the Freudian assertion that what we call agency is in fact founded in the *unconscious* or, in any case, is not represented by what passes for an expression of the *will*. Focusing upon the ostensibly normative character of "interaction" confronted with the "rational autonomy" of scientific method, Lacan argues that: "From the moment man thinks that the great clock of nature turns all by itself, and continues to mark the hour even when he isn't there, the

---

[14] Ernst Cassirer, *An Essay on Man* (New Haven: Yale University Press, 1944) 66.

order of science is born."[15] And while Freud does not figure in any of Turing's writings, similar implications are clearly worked through by him with regard to the materiality of machinic processes and computer literacy.

In this vein, Turing observes that "the fact that Babbage's Analytical Engine was to be entirely mechanical will help us to rid ourselves of a superstition": this superstition being that electronic computers must be in some sense equivalent to the human nervous system and cerebral cortex, as a surrogate for the old idea of "mind" or "transcendental ego" (thereby attempting to smuggle in analogy and the pathetic fallacy by the back door of neurochemical "materialism," while in fact doing little more than dressing the computer up as a type of electronic brain), once more obscuring the question of "intelligence" within the problematic of consciousness, reason and free will. Indeed, the radical materiality of computing processes—which we must also recognise as semiotic processes—reveals a certain paradox in attempts, as Turing says, both to universalise and to "localise" the phenomenon of consciousness.

4. A similar sense of this paradox is provided by Ludwig Wittgenstein in his preliminary studies for the *Philosophical Investigations*. "It is misleading," Wittgenstein writes, "to talk of thinking as of a 'mental' activity. We may say that thinking is essentially the activity of operating with signs. This activity is performed by the hand, when we think by writing; by the mouth and larynx, when we think by speaking; and if we think by *imagining* signs or pictures, I can give you no agent that thinks. If then you say that in such cases the mind thinks, I would only draw your attention to the fact that you are using a *metaphor*, that here the mind is an agent in a different sense from that in which the hand can be said to be an agent in writing."[16] This recalls a familiar anecdote of Albert Einstein's, who—in reference to the advantages of calculating manually on paper in contrast with mental calculus—used to say "my pencil is cleverer than I."[17]

---

[15] Jacques Lacan, "Psychoanalysis and Cybernetics, or On the Nature of Language," *The Seminar of Jacques Lacan. Book II*, 298.

[16] Ludwig Wittgenstein, *The Blue and Brown Books: Preliminary Studies for the Philosophical Investigations* (New York: Harper, 1958) 6-7.

[17] Cited in Karl R. Popper and John C. Eccles, *The Self and its Brain: An Argument for Interactionism* (New York: Springer International, 1977) 208. Popper: "As I wrote many years ago at the very beginning of the debate about computers, a computer is just a glorified pencil. Einstein once said: 'my pencil is cleverer than I.' What he meant could perhaps be put thus: armed with a pencil, we can be more than twice as clever as we are without. Armed with a computer ... we can perhaps be more than a hundred

The question of agency, however, proceeds beyond the assumption of an inner rational actor (an "I" abstracted from the instrumentality of its mere "prostheses"), to the very concept of signification itself: of the relation, as Wittgenstein says, between "thinking" and "operating with signs"; or otherwise between the assumptions of interactivity and the logic and structure of *accountable action*. When Turing contends that "mechanism and writing are from our point of view almost synonymous," he is making a statement not simply about the *action* of writing (such as the mechanism of certain "writing machines," for example the typewriter or Schreibmaschine) but about a generalised technē of inscription—which extends, as Freud points out, to the very structuration of the psychic apparatus and the metaphorics of the written trace in the organisation of perception, memory and cognition. Or as semioticians like Yuri Lotman, and later Thomas Sebeok, have implied; extending to the structuration of all living systems (or "semiospheres"). Indeed, we may say that such a generalised technē describes a condition of *any* dynamic system whatsoever—including a material "system of consciousness" that no longer requires a philosophy of self nor the identification of agency with something like "mind" (nor indeed any type of "organic" phenomenon either).

This would be another way of regarding interactivity as a general structuring principle, or *tropism*, founded upon the "ambivalence" of a between-two-states.[18] That is to say, the ambivalence of a "communication" that is not premised upon the ideality of a direct one-to-one correspondence (stimulus/response; input-output), but is instead underwritten by an arbitrarily defined, causally *differential* relation between otherwise non-coincident cognitive or signifying events—in which, as posited by Saussure, but also implied by Jacques Loeb and I.P. Pavlov, such arbitrary relations describe an emergent structurality that makes the inference of *language* possible, as what may thus be recognised as a network of signs—whether this occurs at a micro- or macro- level; as a binary unit or operating system; phoneme, trope, schema; or the signifying field "as a whole."[19] A similar ambivalence is sug-

times as clever as we are without; and with improving computers there need not be an upper limit to this."

[18] Concerning animal tropisms, and the détournement of external stimulus and resulting response, see Jacques Loeb, *The Mechanical Conception of Life: Biological Essays* (Chicago: University of Chicago Press, 1912) and *Studies in General Psychology* (Chicago: The University of Chicago Press, 1905).

[19] The notion that interactivity or "communication" remains structurally ambivalent is a necessary development from the translational notion of language as a series of codes operating on a one-to-one correspondence with an encoded or "signified" meaning. Cf.

gested by Turing to characterise what we call intelligent behaviour, as distinct from a purely "mechanistic" rationalism. It is perhaps the more interesting feature of signifying systems that the interactivity of its mechanisms gives rise to non-mechanistic functions, very much in the manner of dynamic systems or "information" systems, whereby causal determinacy gives way to "sensitive dependence upon initial conditions." Considerations of this nature had led Turing in the first place to posit computability upon a principle of *undecidability* and to observe that "most of the programmemes which we can put into the machine will result in its doing something that we cannot make sense of at all, or which we regard as completely random behaviour."[20] Such randomness is seen, however, to be largely mimetic in quality, *insofar* as the machine's "behaviour" is measured against humanistic assumptions of intelligence and predictability. But just as Turing implies here a refutation of the idea of "universal intelligence" on any generalised humanistic basis, so does Lacan similarly refute the Cartesian notion of "the machine," along with that of a machine that (actively) *imitates*; that is merely the analogue of an assumed rationality.

For Lacan, there is no object or agent of imitation outside the desire represented to the interrogator by way of the imaginary dimension of the interrogative act itself. Hence Lacan's rejection of behavioural experiments broadly speaking, on the basis that consciousness can only be defined in terms of the mechanical "assumption" of an image (or even of an ad hoc "model of the real"). This, taken in an experimental context, also raises the commonplace problem of the "observer paradox," where the psychologised character of the test's "decision processes" is influenced, and partly formed (entrained), by the testing procedure and by the "subject" implied by and within it (an implied subject which henceforth may be said to describe the *analogue* of a general intelligence).[21] Insofar as the experiment enacts an hypothesis directed at eliminating, constraining or determining the logic of random or variable behaviour, experimental proof or disproof nevertheless claims for itself a validity that remains cogent only within the framework of the experiment. Which is to say, of the experimental *rationale*. Randomness, in this sense, is always affective, or at the very least an operation played out within a supposedly controlled environment whose characteristics are nevertheless assumed to be universal (and thus, in some sense, transcendent; beyond the

Claude Shannon, "A Mathematical Theory of Communication," *Bell System Technical Journal* 27 (July-October, 1948).

[20] Alan Turing, "Computing Machinery and Intelligence," *Mind* LIX.236 (1950): 460.

[21] Cf. Lacan, "A Materialist Definition of the Phenomenon of Consciousness," 41ff.

claims, that is, of any hidden variable). What emerges from this, contrary to assumptions about the character of randomness as supposing some sort of semantic content that can be regularised within a system, is that systematicity itself in fact devolves upon the structural dynamics by which randomness is "permitted" in the first place. Importantly, it is in such a broadly structural-dynamic sense that Lotman argues that "intelligence is always an interlocutor,"[22] where *interlocutor* implies, as Paul Virilio says, a teletechnology "of generalised interactivity,"[23] or what we might call *inter-mediality*, not as causally-defined action—translating between different states and attributing to them a degree of mutual "prediction"—but the *inter* of an action defined as the ambivalent, labile-mechanical *basis* of any assumption of causality or of structure as such.

5. Linked to intellection, we see that the idea of interactivity leads us to posit "agency" as being something like an *operator*—a switching mechanism of a between-two-states—somewhat in the manner of Maxwell's Demon. This hypothetical operator, "mediating" between the so-called subject and an otherwise imaginary interlocutor, is purely schematic and retro-active while nevertheless presenting a model for what amounts to a *generator of discourse* or of what Wittgenstein terms, in the broadest sense, *sign operations*. Posited in reverse, the inter-state logic of Maxwell's Demon models discourse upon a principle of reparation of "differences" (i.e. of discrete states) which remains, however, driven by entropy and by what we might even call a constitutive superpositionality (as we will see later, it is this superpositionality that ultimately renders any *mediation* here imaginary or otherwise affective). At the same time, it is the hypothetical status of this demon that remains central to the generative-discursive process, since there is nothing *of* the demon that may be said to be realised, or realisable, in the form of— say—an embodied intention or intelligence. It remains, instead, on the level of what Wolfgang Iser has called an *emergent*, or what elsewhere has been theorised with regard to the unfigurability of the "event." In this sense, what we refer to when we use the term "agent" is in fact a type of *event-state*: neither an entity nor a reification or concretisation of a prior "programmeme," but rather a programmematic *structural ambivalence*.

---

22 Yuri Lotman, "Culture without Literacy / Culture before Culture," *Universe of the Mind: A Semiotic Theory of Culture*, trans. Ann Shukman (Bloomington: Indiana University Press, 2000) 2.

23 Paul Virilio, "The Third Interval: A Critical Transition," *Rethinking Technologies*, ed. Verena Andermatt Conley (Minneapolis: University of Minnesota Press: 1993) 7.

Consequently, when we speak of a "generalised interactivity," or *discursivity*, as Virilio does, we are in fact speaking of a *condition* of language—or "communication"—and not simply of a *characteristic* of language (so-called mediation, for example). Again, interactivity is not merely a term descriptive of communication processes, but rather of a condition of possibility upon which the phenomenon of such things as inter-subjectivity are ultimately predicated. Indeed, as Lacan has pointed out, subjectivity is constituted as an inter-active *effect*, being not a relation of transmission or communication as such, but rather an open relation of transmissibility and communicability, orientated towards an *other*. Interaction, therefore, is always *predicative* (insofar as it *assumes a relation to an object*, however tentative, evanescent or hypothetical), such that so-called *intersubjectivity* remains both illusory (or "aporetic") and formally equivalent to *reflexivity* (being, as it is, structurally dialogical). The assumed inter-action of, or with, a self and its others hence assumes the form of something like the binary recursive form of a mirror-effect. Moreover, this mirror-effect will always have been one in which the "interactive agent," so called, is not a subject as such, but rather an ambi-*valence* upon which reflexivity—and hence agency—devolves, as its so-called mediating third term in the subject-predicate equation S = P.

With the accelerated "progress" of teletechnologies and hypermediality, the notion of a discrete, or even dialectically structured, subjectivity increasingly gives way to one of radically polyvalent, immersive signifying environments, in which the transverse character of "interactions" no longer affirms or even permits assumptions of subjectivity founded upon the idea of a paradigm of consciousness or rational agency (as opposed, presumably, to an *ir*rational agency). This in turn has implications for how we define "environments" (i.e. as either objective or normative context, situation, or set of parameters, defined for example according to controlled experimentation) and how we posit the limits or contours of interactivity—as something determinate, measurable and thus ideally "testable"—and risks inviting a return to something like a semiotic or cybernetic "metaphysics" (the logic of the programmeme, for example, as paradigmatic and causal, rather than as strictly contingent or conditional). In the generalisation of interactivity, as an event-state of material and mechanical processes, it becomes more and more difficult to assert the (transcendental) claims of a subject as actor, or even of a subject as such, other than as the figure of a "universal interlocutor" posited within and as the tropic condition of mediality itself.

Such risks come increasingly to the fore particularly in those branches of experimental and applied science that seek to transpose the problematic of artificial intelligence onto the effort to map and control human and animal behaviour through direct, physical (electromechanical) control of the brain. An example of this can be found in testimony recorded in the 24 February 1974 edition of the United States *Congressional Record*, by José Delgado—former director of neuropsychiatry at Yale University Medical School—who stated the following:

> We need a programmeme of psychosurgery for political control of our society. The purpose is physical control of the mind. Everyone who deviates from the given norm can be surgically mutilated.
>
> The individual may think that the most important reality is his own existence, but this is only his personal point of view. This lacks historical perspective.
>
> Man does not have the right to develop his own mind. This kind of liberal orientation has great appeal. We must electrically control the brain. Someday, armies and generals will be controlled by electric stimulation of the brain.[24]

Author of *Physical Control of the Mind: Toward a Psychocivilised Society* (1971), Delgado's major methodological innovations included the permanent implantation of electrodes in the brain; intracerebral chemitrodes and dialytrodes; cardiac pacemaker implantation; brain pacemakers; brain radio stimulators; two-way radio communication brain-to-computer; time-lapse recording of social behaviour in monkey colonies; and the design and application of non-invasive electromagnetic devices for the investigation of biological effects and therapeutic application.

It may simply be incidental that Delgado is known to have cooperated with government agencies in Spain and the United States, under Franco and Nixon, with the objective of developing means of direct electro-technical control of psycho-physical activity and thence, ultimately, of individual and social behaviour in general. Yet Delgado's remarks to the US Congress, in the political context of an emergent Soviet "unified information system," draw our attention to an important fact. Just as technology, despite its recent proliferation across all spheres of life, no longer appears *invasive*— rather the contrary—so, too, it no longer appears today as fantastic and ethically suspect to conceive of, or espouse, techniques of control whose invasiveness remains below the threshold of social representability. In other words, the modes of control inherent to new forms of interactive technology remain *incidental*, in a world in which the premise of a "critical media consciousness" tends more and more to *coincide* with, for example, the rapid proliferation of

---

[24] *Congressional Record* 118.26 (1974): 4475.

Chimpanzees Paddy (left) and Carlos at Yale University Medical School, each with two intracerebral electrodes and boxes for instrumentation. From José Delgado, *Physical Control of the Mind: Toward a Psychocivilised Society* (Irvington: 1971).

bio-technologies such as genetic modification, RNAi, cloning, robotics, bionics, global telecommunications and surveillance, and the whole multiplicity of micro-, macro- and nano-technologies. Meanwhile, in the post-Cold War political climate of late 20th-century, technological "accountability"—linked to the aspiration of a public domain—has long vanished behind a new Iron Curtain of international patents and a renewed military-industrial progressivist rhetoric (despite a resurgence during the first years of the 21st-century of moral majoritarianism in the US—with regard to such things as stem-cell research, abortion and the medical use of human embryos—and despite a broad non-US scepticism with regard to the motives of corporations engaged in vivisection, bio-genetics and research into animal or artificial intelligence).

Whether utopia or doomsday scenario, an emergent "technoetic" globalism[25] is effectively reconstituting the very idea of mind, and of "mind control," in ways that even half a century ago would have appeared science fiction, just as it has transformed the critical and ethical paradigms for determining the limits and nature of the so-called "mind problem." The advent of computing science, cy-

---

[25] On technoetics, see Roy Ascott, "The Mind of the Museum," *Telematic Embrace: Visionary Theories of Art, Technology, and Consciousness*, ed. Edward A. Shanken (Berkeley: University of California Press, 2003) 341.

bernetics, systems and information theory in the ten years following WWII, gave rise to the notion that characteristics of mind, and above all "intelligence," could be *affected* by technical means, thereby initiating the most radical phase of industrialisation yet: the industrialisation of "consciousness" and the final transition from machine age to information age—and with it, the renewed contest for global informatic, economic and political hegemony.

In this movement of constant transition, the task remains not only to think the relation of consciousness to technology, and to what we might call the law of supersession, but to discover what is at stake in it beyond the paradigm of "mind control," or what would amount to a *return to reason* by other means. But if the advent of cybernetics implied more than simply a moment of transition in the Spinozan hypothesis, deus sive natura sive machina, it did so to the degree that it posed the problem of the nature-technology dichotomy as *determinate* of any logic of control—of localised or universal reason—that may devolve upon it. That is, of any logic of agency. Between the so-called organic mind and its mechanical counterpart, a genealogy of supersession and recursion appears to underwrite the mental rebus, according to which—even under the most intrusive clinical circumstances—the logic of "control" discloses a base discursivity in what are called the operations of thought.

6. While commentators like McLuhan sought to locate antecedents for the "transition" from machine age to information age in the earlier technologisation of literacy—by way, for example, of the mechanised printing press (the "Gutenberg effect")—and the parallel advent—by way of television and telemedia—of a post-"typographic man," others like Claude Shannon identified within the idea of language itself the technological basis for the changes at hand. In 1948 Shannon published his landmark "A Mathematical Theory of Communication," which established the industry standard of information theory, followed in 1949 by a paper entitled "Communication Theory of Secrecy Systems," in which language is defined as a "stochastic process which produces a discrete sequence of symbols in accordance with some system of probability."[26]

Along with Turing's pioneer work on cryptanalysis, computing and artificial intelligence, Shannon's theoretical papers have provided the basis for rethinking "cognition" in terms of

---

[26] Claude Shannon, "Communication Theory of Secrecy Systems," *Bell System Technical Journal* 28 (October, 1949).

programmematics and recursive codes, and of identifying "information" with effects of disturbance intrinsic to any language system or system of sign operations. The implication here being that programmemes or computing codes, like language, are not simply "error prone," but rather error-determined, with the consequence — as we may better appreciate today — that despite the most rigorous forms of dataveillance every system is inherently susceptible to "viral" interference. Moreover, Shannon's work on communication and unpredictability proved to be one of the major forerunners of more recent "chaos" theories which, along with quantum mechanics and quantum computing, have offered some of the more persuasive accounts of neural event-structures and the constitution of "intelligence" or "mind." In light of such developments, cognitive linguists, like George Lakoff and Gilles Fauconnier, have similarly proposed that language and human thought processes are both "non-logical" and "non-generative," instead being defined by endless idiosyncrasies of patterning and distribution.[27]

Shannon's other major study, *A Symbolic Analysis of Relay and Switching Circuits* (his 1937 masters dissertation at the Massachusetts Institute of Technology), extended the notion of recursive language systems and cryptanalysis to problems dealing with computing and programmematics, by applying Boolean algebra to establish the theoretical underpinnings of digital circuits. This work has had broad significance due to the fact that digital circuits are fundamental to the operation of modern computers and telecommunications systems. As information technologies have become increasingly networked in complex ways, and "intelligent" systems increasingly come to mimic neural structures of parallel processing, the circuit has come to be a paradigm case not only for understanding cognitive structures, but for mapping contemporary social organisation — from the power grids and computerised transit systems that allow our cities to function, to the advent of "global" information systems like GPS and the World Wide Web.

First proposed by Tim Berners-Lee at the Centre Européenne pour la Recherche Nucléaire (CERN) in Geneva in March 1989, and based upon a distributed hypertext system, the World Wide Web has often been regarded as something analogous to a *global mind*, organised across an almost countless array of computing nodes.[28] This idea was foreshadowed in a widely discussed proposal by US science administrator (and former Manhattan Project advisor) Van-

---

[27] See, for example, Gilles Fauconnier, *Mental Spaces: Aspects of Meaning Construction in Natural Languages* (Cambridge: Cambridge University Press, 1994).
[28] See Tim Berners-Lee, "Information Management: A Proposal," CERN (March, 1989).

nevar Bush, entitled "As We May Think" (1945),[29] which called for new, non-linear technical means of managing the industrial output of information—an output dramatically accelerated during WWII. The development of the Web at CERN (building upon the existing global networks of ARPANET and the Internet) was initially prompted by similar concerns about effective information management and the need to discover means of linking remotely distributed information together across heterogeneous systems in an unconstrained way.

As a multi-user system with a radically decentred structure, the Web can more easily be considered analogous to certain non-human "neural structures"—such as those of various types of insects—rather than to the "singular" brain-centredness of humans. Biomimetics has explored structures similar to those of the Web in certain invertebrates and insects, whose compositely localised, networked "intelligence" is comprised of multiple ganglia located across the body, capable of the rapid assimilation and processing of information before it is able to reach a central "brain." In practical terms, this provides the organism with a vastly enhanced reaction time (or what Berners-Lee termed "automatic analysis"), just as the organisation of relay-points and microprocessors is designed to speed up the circulation of "information" in computing circuits, GSM networks, and global positioning (a concept further-radicalised in quantum computing's exploitation of entanglement and non-locality). Similar principles of organisation have been noted in the perceptory systems of locusts and bees, whose multiple lens structures give their optical centres the capacity to isolate photo-effects of extremely high frequencies. In similar ways, biomimetics—which seeks to develop imitative technologies for use by humans (such as the adaptation of ultrasonic devices, like those employed by bats in order to "see" in the dark, as prostheses for blind people)—points to a broad understanding of cognition on the basis of enhanced, networked, pan-sensory (synaesthetic) experience, "re-coded" in human terms as a *real virtuality*—a virtual reality grounded in material phenomena.

7. The manufacture of "mind" has long represented the apotheosis of human technical ambition, whether by way of literacy, philosophy, education or indoctrination, or by various instruments of belief, physical or psychic control and coercion, or by way of technology itself. In the 1930s, W.R. Hess (in Zürich) had devised procedures to implant very fine wires within the brains of anesthe-

---

[29] Vannevar Bush, "As We May Think," *Atlantic Monthly* 176 (July 1945): 101-8.

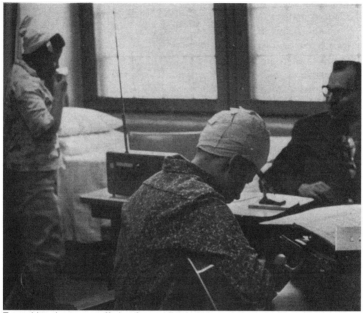

Two girls who were suffering from epileptic seizures and behavioural disturbances requiring implantation of electrodes in the brain for diagnostic and therapeutic purposes. Under the cap, each patient wears a "stimoceiver," used to stimulate the brain by radio and to send electrical signals of brain activity by telemetry while the patients are completely free within the hospital ward. From José Delgado, *Physical Control of the Mind.*

tised cats[30]—a direct antecedent to the later neurophysiological work of Delgado. By the 1950s, the reduced size of electrodes and the invention of micromanipulators made it possible to establish direct communication between brain and computer, circumventing normal sensory organs. In this way, "automatic learning" was discovered to be possible by feeding ELF signals (i.e. Extremely Low Frequencies) directly into specific neuronal structures without the conscious participation of the test subject.

Already in 1971 Delgado was able to write: "The technology for nonsensory communication between brains and computers through the intact skin is already at our fingertips, and its consequences are difficult to predict. In the past the progress of civilisation has tremendously magnified the power of our senses, muscles, and skills. Now we are adding a new dimension: the di-

---

[30] See *Perspectives of Motor Behaviour and its Neural Basis*, eds. M.-C. Hepp-Reymond and G. Marini (Basel: Karger, 1997) 103-134.

rect interface between brains and machines."[31] One of the apparent consequences of direct brain-computer "interaction" is a return, among cyberneticists, to the notion that the mind operates—or can be made to operate—as a type of Cartesian theatre, in which a disembodied ego addresses commands to an otherwise unconscious subject whose *Being* is by reason of its having been *thought in advance*. It is of little consequence whether this ego corresponds to some sort of internal mechanism or to an externalised machine; what matters is that the ideological command structure represented by this phantasmatic "disembodied ego" is implanted—directly or by way of a system of transmissions—into the physical brain. The Cartesian subject is thus subtly transformed through a hybridisation of media that, even as it employs the tropes of mentalistic "acts," "control" or "reason," effects a turn towards post-biological systems of "cyberception" in which the analogy of the Cartesian theatre collapses into the cyclical recursions of what McLuhan termed the "rear-view mirror" effect of supersessive media, and what Roy Ascott has termed—in reference to Bateson's "mind at large"—*telenoia*: "networked consciousness, interactive awareness, thought at a distance."[32] The dichotomy of mind and matter is not only rendered fictive, but it is precisely this fictive element that the "subject" will never be able to pin down as representing for it the controlling power behind its relation to "its own" thinking. Which also means, to its own Being—affecting, thereby, something like the *real absence* of a phantom limb.

In a sense, what is demonstrated here is that, as Freud and Lacan had long before anticipated, the "core of our Being does not *coincide* with the ego."[33] It, the ego, is "something else"—"an object which fills a certain [...] imaginary function"—upon the basis of which the illusion of Cartesian subjectivity (of its syllogistic necessity, its interpolated *ergo*) is able to sustain itself despite all evidence pointing to the fact that it itself is already decentred; that its Being is something both antecedent *and* consequent, externalised, *prosthetic*. In this way also, the imaginary ego or "operator" comes to represent a foreign body or alien influence whose very possibility implies that what is called *mind* in some sense already, and necessarily, stands in an open relation to both an "operational" materiality and to unconscious "command"—hence situating the so-called subject as a figure of contingency and ambivalence (as we see in Freud) for whom "resistance" and "emancipation," for

[31]   José Delgado, *Physical Control of the Mind: Toward a Psychocivilized Society* (New York: Harper & Row, 1969) 95.
[32]   Ascott, "The Architecture of Cyberception," *Telematic Embrace*, 325.
[33]   Lacan, "A Materialist Definition of the Phenomenon of Consciousness," 44.

instance, are finally objectifiable only in the sense that they imply a relation to the real concretised as an experience of a *lapsus*. That is to say, related to a reflexivity or circuit of transmission and inter-mission; of "automatic analysis" and "inter-action."[34]

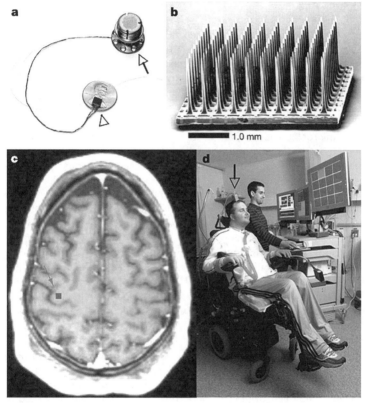

Intracortical sensor and placement, participant 1. From Hochberg *et al.*, "Neuronal ensemble control," *Nature* 442 (13 July 2006).

The imaginary function of this ego could thus be said to veil the operations of what is generalised under the term "machine" (here either computer *or* brain), where, as Lacan says, "the machine is the structure detached from the *activity* of the subject." Detached, that is, from anything like an inaugurating will or reason (that

---

[34] Similarly, Lacan notes that what is called an "intersubjective relation, which is the foundation not only of behaviour, but of actions and passions ... has *nothing to do* with consciousness" ("A Materialist Definition of the Phenomenon of Consciousness," 49—emphasis added).

which *acts* under some "metaphysical" compulsion, we might say, and thus "determines"). This, however, does not mean that the machine, for Lacan, remains external to the true *nature* of man, or human reason, rather that technicity—as such—has nothing to do with assumptions of "a philosophy issuing directly from the cogito." Again, the "I think" is here not a cause but a recursivity. Such conclusions have tended—unsurprisingly—to be supported by more recent research focused not only on the transmission of commands *to* the brain, but on the mapping and recognition of neural functions in order to translate brain activity into physical action and thus to produce recursive patterns of digital "interaction." A report published in the science journal *Nature* (13 July 2006) describes how a research team, led by John Donoghue at Brown University, succeeded in implanting a silicon chip studded with microelectrodes—part of a system named BrainGate—into a human subject's primary motor cortex, permitting signals from the brain to be "translated" into computational commands. Additionally, experimentation has further demonstrated that the brain, beyond merely accommodating the neural implant, is effectively able to assimilate (or become technoetically entangled with) an otherwise external, prosthetic device, be it a machine *or* software, which the subject is then able to "operate" with a degree of unconsciousness comparable to that with which normal motor functions are performed.[35] Such assimilation is shown to occur not simply on the level of behavioural modification (movement, *kinēsis*, or reflexive learning), but on a more fundamentally material or *metabolic* level, constitutive of what we might call a generalised "neurotechnology." In this vein, William Ross Adey at the UCLA Brain Research Institute has noted that the external transmission of modulated ELF waves (below 300 hertz), directed at various centres in the brain, is likewise capable of altering internal electroencephalographic patterns, which thus become "entrained."[36] Similar effects of neuroplasticity have been observed in

---

[35] Leigh R. Hochberg, Mijail D. Serruya, Gerhard M. Friehs, Jon A. Mukand, Maryam Saleh, Abraham H. Caplan, Almut Branner, David Chen, Richard D. Penn and John P. Donoghue, "Neuronal ensemble control of prosthetic devices by a human with tetraplegia," *Nature* 442 (13 July 2006): 164-171. This paper reported on a 9-month experiment with test subject Matthew Nagle, a tetraplegic who received the first trial of the 96-electrode BrainGate implant in his right precentral gyrus (motor cortex (MI) for arm).

[36] Cf. K. Kamikawa, J.T. McIlwain, W.R. Adey, "Response Patterns of Thalamic Neurons during Classical Conditioning," *ECG Clininical Neurophysiology* 17.485-496 (1964); and A.R. Sheppard, S.M. Bawin and W.R. Adey, "Models of Long-range Order in Cerebral Macromolecules: Effects of sub-ELF and of Modulated VHF UHF Fields," *Radio Science* 15 (6S) (1979): 141-145. It is important here to keep in view the status of entrainment in terms of classical behaviourist interventions and the consequent inducement of both automatic and contradictory stimulus-response, or causally

experiments concerning synchronisation or quantum entanglement between neural activity and electro-magnetic stimuli (and not only *direct* stimuli but also isolated, discrete circuits), strongly implying that human-computer interfaces may be considered *recursive* in the fullest sense—that interactivity is thus *proprioceptive* and *integrational*—affecting what is for all intents and purposes a neuroprosthetic *system*.

It may be this feature that ultimately prevents the Cartesian notion of a "theatre of the mind"—in which agency is effected by way of a kind of hidden puppeteer or diabolus ex machina—from re-entering the science and philosophy of mind by way of an incomplete cybernetics. One of the legacies of Delgado's and Donoghue's projects is hence that, while no consensus yet exists as to what objectively constitutes "mind," we are nevertheless confronted at every juncture with its technological *invention*. That is to say, what is called mind remains inseparable from a certain emergent inter-activity or "intersticial" technē. This has led—in an apparent restatement of Turing's test hypothesis—to the idea that what is called mind is nothing other than an effect of techno-symbiosis, mediated discursively by particular neural networks or "structural properties." Consequently mind—as an object of enquiry—has assumed a primarily imaginary or analogical character, based upon a limited capacity to represent an experiential or causal relation between so-called processes of intellection and any given environment, or to theorise about other forms of experience beyond the limits of the human sensorium (or of the human *categories* of, for example, organic and inorganic; metabolism and kinēsis; physis and psychē) vis-à-vis a generalised "interface ecology." In treating what amount to a set of biotechnological aporias, questions necessarily also arise as to the task of determining the practical and ethical limits of "what" it is that *mind* represents for us, beyond the contingencies or strategic interventions of "science": be it in terms of free will, consciousness, or civil liberty (even while such terms are complicated by any materialist definition of conscious, or by the admission of a determining, *unconscious* agency at work in the life-world of man). And while the philosophy of mind may have evolved on the basis of a false premise—the desire to explain the seemingly mysterious qualities

conditioned "reflexes"—which reveals not only the effectively arbitrary *orientation* of causal interaction, but an antecedent structure of possibility that allows causal events to firstly arise, and secondly to arise on the basis of an *arbitrarily given state of affairs* (as, for example, so-called "suggestion" during hypnotic states and its physiological interpretation); hence delimiting the extrinsic grounds of behaviourist research. Cf. I.P. Pavlov, *Conditioned Reflexes: An Investigation of the Psychological Activity of the Cerebral Cortex*, trans. G.V. Anrep (New York: Dover, 1960 [1926]) 406ff.

of experience and intellection—it may be that there is nothing *other* than this "false premise"; that mind is constituted solely in the technological interface of the representable and the unrepresentable, on the cusp of verifiability, analogy, metaphor or mimēsis, or as the division between that which thinks and that which makes thinking possible.

Stephen Dougherty

New Media's Body

Embodiment has become an indispensable keyword for cultural studies in the age of virtual reality and digital media. This is a striking fact given that twenty years ago, even ten years ago, there was a ready audience for "visionaries" claiming that digital media heralded a new politics of radical disembodiment. For an idealist posthumanist like Hans Moravec, virtual reality was the first big step in the mind's final overcoming of the body:

> Today's virtual adventurers do not fully escape the physical world: if they bump into real objects, they feel real pain. That link may weaken when direct connections to the nervous system become possible, leading perhaps to the old science-fiction idea of a living brain in a vat. The brain would be physically sustained by life-support machinery, and mentally by connections of all the peripheral nerves to an elaborate simulation of not only a surrounding world but also a body for the brain to inhabit.[1]

As Moravec suggests, the brain in the vat is actually an old science fiction idea. In spirit at least it goes back to Descartes's *Meditations on First Philosophy*, where the deep-thinking philosopher feared that an evil demon might be controlling his seemingly unmediated perceptions of the world; and it goes on up to recent pop culture treatments like *The Matrix*, where the synapses of a million enslaved human brains are kept firing away on simulated sensory input to meet the evil overlords' energy needs. But Moravec goes even further than *The Matrix*, imagining the dematerialisation of the brain along with everything else: "The virtual life of a brain in a vat can still be subtly perturbed by external physical, chemical, or electrical effects impinging on the vat. Even these weak ties to the physical world would fade if the brain, as well as the body, was

---

[1] Hans Moravec, *Robot: Mere Machine to Transcendent Mind* (Oxford: Oxford University Press, 1999) 191.

absorbed into the simulation."[2] It is no less science fiction than *The Matrix*, even if we are supposed to consume this vision of a blissfully brainless world as a credible forecast offered by a serious futurist. Of course it is not credible. In spite of the internet, virtual reality, mixed reality; in spite of the decline of physical-index media and the rise of a new politics of digitalism in aesthetics, philosophy, communications, entertainment, and so on, we still have our bodies, and it is hard to imagine doing without them.

Moravec was wrong. Yet his arguments still have value, at least insofar as they have helped to spur critical and theoretical debate about the *role* of embodiment in digital media. If we still need our bodies, what is the nature of our embodied connection to digital media? *How* is our materiality connected to the materialities of new media? The theorists I want to investigate ask such questions because they are not transcendentalists like Moravec. But neither are they anti-humanists like the German media scientist Friedrich Kittler. While they share Kittler's critical focus on the material dimensions of media, they draw different conclusions about our relation to those media. For Kittler, our era of "digital convergence" signals the point at which information starts going its own way. What Kittler foresees in digital convergence is a world where human perception no longer matters because it will have been displaced by the inhuman circuit of purely symbolic information. Having gone digital, information, both reified and deified as "absolute knowledge," will have transcended the human figure. Digital convergence for Kittler thus denotes a process whereby information, or symbol, or sign, becomes unmoored from any human framework. It's not Moravec, but it *is The Matrix*.

Getting back to the subject more at hand, the theorists I am interested in wish to understand cyberspace, virtual reality, and the world of digital images both in terms of their material dimensions (unlike Moravec), and in terms of our embodied engagements with them (unlike Kittler). As Laura Marks suggests, "[t]o appreciate the materiality of our media pulls us away from a symbolic understanding and toward a shared physical existence."[3] In light of the slightly ridiculous and vaguely menacing positions surveyed above,[4] such

---

[2] Moravec, *Robot*, 192.

[3] Laura U. Marks, *Touch: Sensuous Theory and Multisensory Media* (Minneapolis: University of Minnesota Press, 2002) xii.

[4] These anti-humanist discourses have their own distinct emphases. While Moravec underscores the immateriality of the digital, Kittler stresses the opposite. As Paul Taylor and Jan Harris explain, "Kittler's account stresses the materiality of communication—it emphasises how the digital is material and involves a complexification of matter rather than its transcendence" (Paul A. Taylor and Jan L.I. Harris, *Digital Matters: The Theory and Culture of the Matrix* [London: Routledge, 2005] 86). But the place of the human in the era of digital media is just as tenuous for Kittler as it is for

appreciation is extremely important. It is a strategy for making humans matter as an integral part of our communications circuits.

Yet note the striking contrast Laura Marks sets up in the passage quoted above. If we really wish to understand "the materiality of our new media," and if we truly seek to know how our human bodies fit into the circuit of information that seems so inhuman at least on the surface, then we must give up on "symbolic understanding." If we do that, Marks concludes, we can more fully commit ourselves to the political good of our shared existence. Where does this idea come from: that the world of symbols, or signifiers, gets in the way of our shared experiences? It is of a piece with the ancient maxim that silence is golden, that words and gestures are an inadequate substitute for the expression of what lies beyond words and gestures. More specifically, given the theoretical context in which Marks's statement is made, it is part of a backlash against the linguistically oriented constructivism that has dominated cultural studies in recent decades. Marks wishes to give back to the material body something of the agency that has been ignominiously stripped from it under the constructivist paradigm. However, if Kittler turns the symbolic register into a voracious monster ready to take over the universe, spitting out human beings with their outmoded perceptual ratios along the way, this theoretical abandonment of the symbolic dimension that Marks's statement hints at might go too far in the opposite direction. Maybe turnabout is fair play. But must the rehabilitation of embodiment for cultural studies necessarily entail the abjection of the symbolic? Perhaps the answer is yes, because perhaps the ramifications of the global information culture are threatening enough that the life of the body *should* be theoretically decoupled from that of language. That does, however, seem to play into the hands of the anti-humanists, who argue from a similar assumption, where our *embodied existence* is imagined as being jeopardised by the symbol-manipulating powers of computers.

Here, then, is the guiding question of this brief essay: What are the effects of this abjection of language in cultural and media studies? The very question might be grossly premature, since the contemporary turn in these disciplines to updated varieties of phenomenology and related theories of affect is new indeed. What is more, the question is emotionally loaded: to speak of the abjection of language is a strong way of putting it, and perhaps what we are

Moravec. Taylor and Harris continue: "In Kittler's vision, society is a material media matrix, not in the sense of a society ruled by simulation or spectacle, but rather at the deepest structural level. The question remains of what the role of human beings becomes in this scenario" (86).

really talking about is a matter of shifting emphasis along a continuum. "Many kinds of objects and events mean, in many heterogeneous ways and contexts," writes Eve Kosofsky Sedgwick in *Touching Feeling*, "and I see some value in not reifying or mystifying the linguistic kinds of meaning unnecessarily."[5] Sedgwick's implication is that the cultural theory of the last several decades has been marked precisely by such linguistic reification of meaning, and that is good reason for us to begin taking non-linguistic meaning-making far more seriously in our critical calculations. The theorist I shall focus on in this essay, Mark Hansen, would surely justify his work in a similar fashion; and yet his practice would belie something else: an implacable attitude toward the linguistic, a hard turn to what Maurice-Merleau-Ponty called our "motor significance" and our "motor being"[6] such that it slides toward a motor reification that is in some ways exemplary, and that demands close critical attention.

Rather than seeing bodies as either reducible to a universal and digitised currency of information or left out of the information loop altogether by virtue of the digital's autonomy, Mark Hansen understands the organic structure of the body as the "'place' where the self-differing of media gets concretised"[7]; the place, in other words, where the digital metamorphoses into something both sensual and meaningful in spite of its origin in electric nothingness and numerical-symbolic abstraction. This is what makes new media new according to Hansen. New media needs the human body as the enframer of information that is de-specified through its digitisation.[8]

In order to correlate new media with what he calls "a strong theory of embodiment," in *New Philosophy for New Media*, Hansen turns to Henri Bergson's theory of perception (*NP* 3). For Bergson, as Hansen explains, the body acts as "a kind of filter that selects, from among the universe of images circulating around it and ac-

---

[5] Eve Kosofsky Sedgwick, *Touching Feeling: Affect, Pedagogy, Performativity* (Durham: Duke University Press, 2003) 6.

[6] Maurice Merleau-Ponty, *Phenomenology of Perception*, trans. Colin Smith (London: Routledge, 2002) 211.

[7] Mark B.N. Hansen, *New Philosophy for New Media* (Cambridge, Mass.: MIT Press, 2004) 31; hereafter cited in the text as *NP*.

[8] Hansen writes: "We could say, to put it in simple terms, that it is the body—the body's scope of perceptual and affective possibilities—that informs the medial interfaces. This means that with the flexibility brought by digitisation, *there occurs a displacement of the framing function of medial interfaces back onto the body from which they themselves originally sprang*. It is this displacement that makes new media art 'new'" (*NP* 22).

cording to its own embodied capacities, precisely those that are relevant to it." Perception is neither representational nor primarily cognitive: vision is not constituted by a disembodied mind that represents the world to itself; it is constituted by a body/mind/brain that selects, or subtracts, a subset of the ongoing flux of images that make up the world. Thus the body on Bergson's account has great creative power, in large part because it is also a source of action. In its action and movement, in its sensorimotor dimension, it opens up the ontological space for its own self-differing. Drawing heavily on theories of affect from Bergson to Brian Massumi, Hansen explains:

> Insofar as the sensorimotor nexus of the body opens it to its own indeterminacy, it is directly responsible for the body's constitutive excess over itself. In this respect, motion features as the concrete trigger of affection as an active modality of bodily action. In what follows, I shall call this "affectivity": the capacity of the body to experience itself as "more than itself" and thus to deploy its sensorimotor power to create the unpredictable, the experimental, the new. [NP 7]

Hansen uses this basic but far-reaching insight first to correct Deleuze's claim in his books on cinema that the body comprises nothing more than "the passive correlate of linkages between images." (NP 7). If for Deleuze the montage cut and the frame take over the body's role as the "centre of indetermination;" that is, for Deleuze they possess the power to function as purely technical substitutes for the form-giving capacities of the body, for Hansen this is inaccurate. Rather, he argues that the body in its framing function *always* lies behind the operation of the technical frame:

> the frame in any form—the photograph, the cinematic image, the video signal, and so on—cannot be accorded the autonomy Deleuze would give it since its very form (in any concrete deployment) reflects the demands of embodied perception [...]. [NP 8]

The onset of digitisation throws such research findings in starker relief insofar as it dissolves the formerly concrete, media-specific stability of the technical image. The digital is by no means indexical, and the digital image "can no longer be understood as a fixed and objective viewpoint on 'reality'—whether it be theorised as frame, window, or mirror—since it is now defined precisely through its almost complete flexibility and addressability, its numerical basis, and its constitutive 'virtuality'" (NP 8). If some critics and theorists see the end of the image—and the end of the medium—in these developments, Hansen sees the empowerment of the body as the all the more vital enframer of a world of images that have lost their frame.

The aim for Hansen in *New Philosophy for New Media* is to refute Kittler, and to expose the insidious myth of *The Matrix*, the myth of a world of communication that no longer needs human communicators. If Kittler's prophet from the early years of the computer era is Claude Shannon, Hansen turns to lesser known, alternative information theorists for inspiration, such as Donald MacKay. As Hansen explains, the ascendancy and hegemony of Shannon's statistical model of communication theory depended on the suppression of MacKay's, precisely because MacKay, as Hansen notes, sought to preserve "the autonomy of the nontechnical" (*NP* 78) over and against Shannon—and over and against the whole corporatist, rationalist, technocratic thrust of post-World War II speculation about communications. Unlike Shannon, MacKay understood communications as a two-sided process. One side involves the selection of messages from a set in Shannon's sense; the other side involves the construction of meaning out of "everything that goes to make up the biological and cultural specificity of this or that singular receiver" (*NP* 80). Like Bergson, in other words, MacKay argued that a human dimension is always needed to function as a kind of catalyst for the technical dimension.

Given his theoretical motives, Hansen's appropriation of MacKay is sensible, and productive too insofar as it underscores the need to understand technical selection in terms of underlying structure. However, his attempted rehabilitation of the French philosopher Raymond Ruyer is another matter, and in my mind it points to what is an impoverished concept of structure in *New Philosophy*. Like MacKay, Ruyer berated the cybernetics movement of the 1950s for its dual rejection of embodiment and meaning. More pointedly, he criticised cybernetics for comparing information machines to nervous systems. His efforts to correct cybernetics involved a theory of the co-evolution of humans and technology wherein technology is deemed as "intrinsic to the human (and to the living more generally)" (*NP* 81). In place of man-versus-machine dualism on one hand and man-as-machine reductivism on the other, Ruyer proposed a complex, nested hierarchy of organic and machinic components in the order of human life. This hierarchy privileges both a "primary," or organic consciousness, and a "secondary," or human consciousness over machines that Ruyer likewise split off into two distinct kinds: "organic" machines and "mechanical" machines. Following from this move, Ruyer argued that any technical circuit, no matter how autonomous it may seem, always has encoded in it as a kind of spiritual residue the trace of the human consciousness from which it originates. In just the same manner, human consciousness is correlated to the organic consciousness that is its source. The result is that "there is no machine function without the form of conscious life from which it emerges" (NP 81).

For Ruyer, what gives consciousness the power to frame the technical is that it moves in a dimension where machines do not. The conscious organism possesses a machinic dimension, since its nervous circuits are essentially little electrical switches. However, that doesn't mean that the organism is a machine in itself. As an organism it also encompasses another dimension, what Ruyer calls the "transpatial" or "axiological" dimension. Hansen explains:

> As a nonobservable x—a being capable of what Ruyer calls an "absolute survey" or pure "self-enjoyment"—the organism thus enjoys a nonempirical or transpatial existence, an absolute experience of itself that is not accessible to an observer and not constitutable as a scientific object. Insofar as it is responsible for informing the physical with meaning, this transpatial domain constitutes the source of information: it is what produces information on the basis of meaning, that is, from out of a transpatial domain of themes and values. [NP 183]

What Ruyer calls absolute survey and self-enjoyment, Hansen also refers to as "a nondimensional grasping of a perceptual field as an integral whole [...]" (NP 163). In spite of the altered vocabulary, given the fact that Hansen, following Ruyer, insists on the absolute priority of this dimension for meaning-making, it is hard not to read in it a suspicious desire: a return to a firm basis, an originary ground from which we might build a body-oriented subjectivism to substitute for a debunked Cartesian subjectivism. "The bottom line," Hansen writes, "is that we are able to perceive images only because we sense ourselves as form. Perception, in short, depends on affectivity. What this means is that the auto-subjectivity of form-giving forms cannot be likened to a perception of self, but must be understood as a primary affectivity, a 'consciousnss texture,' that underlies and conditions all experience, including perceptual experience" (NP 176-7). Hansen's project is contemporary in terms of its theoretical inputs, yet it is also philosophically conservative. In fact, it is deeply romantic. As the above passage suggests, it pays homage to something very much like Rousseau's "beau sauvage," the primitive body capable of enjoying a distinctly individuated, auto-affective, pre-social existence. If digital information displaces the body in various ways in The Matrix, Moravec, and Kittler, here it's the other way around. The concept of a mediating symbolic register gets swallowed up into the body in its absolute self-presence and its self-enjoyment.

Hansen's theorisation of the frame in his media studies evokes not only Deleuze, but Heidegger as well. As we have seen, Hansen argues that the technically generated symbols, or signifiers, that constitute digital information must necessarily be enframed by the life of the human body if they are to be rendered meaningful. Hansen thus turns Heidegger's theory of enframement on its head, since Heidegger insisted that enframement works the other way around: that it is human beings who are always already enframed by technology and symbolisation. Heidegger's theory of enframement supposes a strong degree of technological and linguistic determination, as expressed in the key metaphor of the prison house of language. In contrast, Hansen's version of enframement in *New Philosophy for New Media* supposes a unity and integrity of pre-linguistic experience that harkens back to Maurice Merleau-Ponty rather than Heidegger. In other words, Hansen's fundamental precepts come from the sort of phenomenological humanism of the mid-twentieth century that poststructuralism, drawing its inspiration in no small part from Heidegger, sought to deconstruct and deligitimate. In this manner, Hansen's attempted movement beyond such theory—indeed, beyond "theory," as the term is generally used in the humanities—involves a recovery of what "theory" rejected in its constitution; and if theory as it became popularly practiced in the intervening decades *was* too caught up for its own good in a world of words, seemingly unable to verify from behind the prison walls that there is anything but words, *New Philosophy* threatens another kind of prison house: that of our mute embodiment cut off from the world, and cut off precisely because it is so insistently privileged in its motor function as the solid ground of the world. In *Bodies in Code*, his second book in a proposed trilogy on new media and embodiment, Hansen reformulates his theory of enframement in a manner that is responsive to this kind of objection. He attempts, in other words, to open up the body to the world of objects and other bodies without which, of course, one cannot really speak of auto-affect. Yet how can one speak of this communication or this auto-affect at all without reference to the field of language and the part that it plays in the differential, boundary-making practices by which our embodied agency is constituted? Even though Hansen downplays the role of the "body image," his theory of embodied technicity is all the more image-based.

Hansen's modified thesis in *Bodies in Code* lays stress on the "co-functioning of embodiment with technics,"[9] the ontological insinuation of technics at the very core of our embodiment. "Forging such a cultural image of the body is crucial," Hansen explains,

> if we are to forestall the instrumentalisation of the body and all that follows from it, above all on the foreclosure of being-with or the finitude of our form of life. Far from being a mere "instrument" or the first "medium" (as some versions of posthumanism allege), the body is a primordial and active source of resistance—as the "living expression of something simultaneously organisation and obstacle to its organisation"—that the body forms the source of excess supporting all levels of constitution (or individuation), from the cellular to the cosmic. As source of excess, the body possesses a flexibility that belies any effort, such as that of cyber-cultural criticism (and behind it, of social constructivism), to reduce it to a passive surface for social signification. [*BC* 15]

Technics is already deep down inside of us. This modified ontology might help to retroactively inoculate the argument of *New Philosophy* against the charge of an embodied metaphysics. What is more, it helps Hansen to clarify his opposition to the constructivist paradigm, where the body's agency is subordinated "to the content of the social images that ... open up the space of its exercise" (*NP* 13). The body is irreducible "to a passive surface for social signification" because social images do not possess the power to shape the contours of our embodiment. Or rather, they possess such power only indirectly; they work only *through* the organism's operational power to reorganise itself in response to external perturbations. Our power of imaging is a fundamental existential power. This difference represents the nub of a theoretical gulf between an exhausted constructivism on one hand and a vigorous new phenomenology on the other. For Hansen the limitation of social constructivist theories is that they ultimately fail to "think agency as materialisation" (*NP* 255). Even if Judith Butler's work is the "least guilty" of this failure (which does not save it from especially harsh condemnation), "in the final instance" it "privileges the visual and the objectifying role of the gaze" (*NP* 255).

Hansen offers his autopoetically inspired model of embodied agency as an alternative to poststructuralist mirror games. His strategy involves the strict subordination of body image (social images) to body schema, which is essentially the realm of affect. He strictly subordinates the observational perspective to the operational perspective; the objective to the subjective, surface to depth.

---

9 Mark B.N. Hansen, *Bodies In Code: Interfaces With Digital Media* (New York: Routledge, 2006) 9; hereafter cited in the text as *BC*.

What seems clear from the start, however, is that removing the mirrors leads to rather new problems. As in the following passage, the body suddenly disappears:

> We are therefore, like all beings, pure subjectivities. Our organism (excluding the nervous system) is a set of subjectivities of a different order from conscious subjectivity. We are an object only in appearance; our body is an object only abstractly, in the subjectivity of those who observe us [...]. We are not, and other beings are not any more than us, really incarnate. Mind-body dualism is illusory *because we do not have a body*. [cited in *BC* 11]

What should we make of this? Let me note first that these are not Hansen's words. They belong to Ruyer, though they are quoted appreciatively by Hansen probably for the continuity they help to provide between *New Philosophy* and *Bodies in Code*, and for the connection they help him to forge between his (it must be said) extremely distinctive phenomenological project and the autopoetics with which he will ally it. But back to the words: given that the whole point is to rescue embodied agency for philosophy and cultural studies, they certainly seem bizarre quoted in this context. Hansen immediately qualifies Ruyer's statement in terms of the distinction between the body and embodiment. The idea of embodiment as experienced from the inside does not preclude the body; rather, it encompasses the relation with the body as observed from the outside. Nevertheless, the nod to Ruyer is in my mind most inauspicious. Hansen's goal is to show how digital technology can recall us to our fundamental and irreducible sociality. But he begins by arguing in the strongest terms possible, in a kind of zero-sum fashion, for the absolute priority of affect. Hansen's challenge is thus to theorise our embodied technicity not only in the absence of the linguistic dimension that impoverishes it in its capture, but also in the absence of the very bodies that objectively verify its being-with.

But how can this be? How can Hansen proceed in this fashion? Perhaps we can glean clues by investigating more closely what Hansen means by "bodies in code." On the surface, at any rate, these words would seem to suggest common cause with the digitally besotted posthumanisms that Hansen makes an obvious point of distancing himself from in the passage quoted at the beginning of this section. The "body in code," he writes, does "not mean a purely informational body or a digital disembodiment of the everyday body." Instead, it "mean[s] a body submitted to and constituted by an unavoidable and empowering technical deterritorialisation—a body whose embodiment is realised, and can only be realised, in conjunction with technics" (*BC* 20). Since we know that for Hansen technics is situated outside language (and that poststructuralism's failure is its treatment of technics "as an 'opacity' internal to language,"[10] this technical deterritorialisation is only conceivable in terms of images and image-processing. "[C]oupling with the domain of social images occurs *from within the operational perspective* of the organism and thus comprises a component of its primordial embodied agency" (*BC* 13). The central role of the image in and for our embodiment is the lynchpin in Hansen's work, and it importantly qualifies his professed commitments to the materiality of the body. Even though the image is theorised under the sign of the tactile, in keeping with Hansen's haptic understanding of vision, we find ourselves lurching toward Moravec: "Embodied disembodiment [...] forms a strict complement to the ontology of mixed reality conditioning all real experience. Just as all virtual reality is mixed reality, so too is all embodied life constitutively disembodied" (*BC* 93).

In his essay "Division of the Gaze, or, Remarks on the Color and Tenor of Contemporary Theory," Stephen Melville remarks that theorists of vision from Goethe all the way to Derrida and Lyotard (with Heidegger, Lacan, and Merleau-Ponty in the middle of the roster) have all assumed a relation between vision and language: "all take it that there is a direct connection between what they want to say about vision and the question of its saying or writing. That is, they argue that the writing that would show what is to be seen about vision cannot advance itself as either transparent or reflective in the usual way."[11] Merleau-Ponty's struggle to determine the place of language in our embodied experience is surely testament to its importance for phenomenology.

He saw the philosophical danger in turning language into a god. "Language is a life, is our life and the life of all things," he wrote in *The Visible and the Invisible*. "Not that *language* takes possession of life and reserves it for itself: what would there be to say if there existed nothing but things said? It is the error of the semantic philosophies to close up language as if it spoke only of itself: language lives only from silence [...]."[12] And yet he recognised the impor-

---

[10] See Mark B.N. Hansen, "Reclearing the Ground," *Electronic Book Review*: www.electronicbookreview.com.

[11] Stephen Melville, "Division of the Gaze, or, Remarks on the Colour and Tenor of Contemporary Theory," *Vision in Context: Historical and Contemporary Perspectives on Sight* (London: Routledge, 1996) 111.

[12] Maurice Merleau-Ponty, *The Visible and the Invisible*, trans. Alphonso Lingis. (Evanston: Northwestern University Press, 1968) 125-6; hereafter cited as *VI*.

tance of his contemporary Jacques Lacan, even as he resisted the linguistic turn that chiefly characterised Lacan's new Freudianism:

> the philosopher knows better than anyone that what is lived is lived-spoken, that, born at this depth, language is not a mask over Being, but—if one knows how to grasp it with all its roots and all its folia-tion—the most valuable witness to Being, that it does not interrupt an immediation that would be perfect without it, that the vision it-self, the thought itself, are, as has been said, "structured as a language." [*VI* 126]

On the one hand, Merleau-Ponty thinks of language as nothing more than "witness to Being," even if it is the most valuable wit-ness there is. On the other hand, he seems willing to acknowledge that "vision itself" may indeed be "structured as a language." He alludes to Lacan's dictum that the unconscious is structured like a language. If we pursue the line of the reference, then it seems that what Merleau-Ponty is actually referring to here is what subtends vision: the invisible, or what he called in his late ontology the flesh of the world. In Merleau-Ponty's words, "the presence of the world is precisely the presence of its flesh to my flesh" (*VI* 127). The flesh is the medium of our belonging: "the thickness of the flesh between the seer and the thing is constitutive for the thing of its visibility as for the seer of his corporeity; it is not an obstacle be-tween them, it is their means of communication" (*VI* 135).

For Hansen, the supreme political and aesthetic value of digital technologies is in their potential to incarnate this flesh, to *be* this flesh in and as a kind of virtual intensification of itself as media, or the phenomenon of mediation. VR and other digital technologies, he writes, "create a rich, anonymous 'medium' for our enactive co-belonging, or 'being-with' one another [...] (*BC* 20). Yet what he refuses to brook is the possibility that Merleau-Ponty leaves open, almost like an invitation, in spite of the distance between his ontol-ogy and Lacan's: that this flesh which is "is the coiling over of the visible upon the seeing body" (*VI* 146) is inextricably bound to-gether with the life of language. Hansen's failure to acknowledge this is all the more striking in light of the powerful and obvious fact of which he seems to be totally aware, and yet somehow oblivious at the same time—that it is language, or code, that subtends the image in digital technology. In which case, as Hartmut Winkler writes, "technology itself has to be conceptualised as a code, that is, as a condensed social deposit that is capable of determining subsequent practices [...]."[13] Hansen's new media theory would be a more effective instrument if it did allow this, but it would mean thinking together and weighing in more value-neutral terms many of the binary elements that he sunders, up to and including the digital and the analogue.

[13] Hartmut Winkler, "Discourses, Schemata, Technology, Monuments: Outline for a Theory of Cultural Continuity," *Technicity*, eds. Arthur Bradley and Louis Armand (Prague: Litteraria Pragensia, 2006) 150.

Roy Ascott

Terror Incognito:
Steps Toward an Extremity of Mind

Reductionist alert! A health warning to our friends in the reductionist camp: artists will look anywhere, into any discipline, scientific
or spiritual, any view of the world, however extreme or esoteric,
any culture, immediate or distant in space or time, any technology,
ancient or modern, in order to find ideas and processes which allow
for untrammelled navigation of mind, and the open-ended exploration of consciousness. We recognise no meta-language or meta-
system that places one discipline or world-view automatically
above all others. This is why we look in all directions for inspiration
and understanding: to the East as well as the West; the left hand
path as well as the right; working with both reason and intuition,
sense and nonsense, subtlety and sensibility. It is a transdiscipli-
nary syncretism that best informs artistic research, just as it is
cyberception that enables our focus on multiple realities, and technoetic instrumentality that supports our self-creation, and our
telematic distribution of presence and re-configuration of identity.
Fundamentalist Materialists may find some content of this text of-
fensive.

Earlier societies approached unknown lands, the terra incognito
of the unmapped planet, with fearful caution. Citizens in many
states today view their own cities with similar fearfulness, as a
terror incognito, in the face, not only of terrorist threats from unknown quarters but of the very provisions claimed to ensure their
civic safety—intensive surveillance, where every public space is
monitored by police cameras, arbitrary powers of arrest for reasons
unstated and unknown, indefinite imprisonment without trial, state
approved torture—signalling the emergence of a political environ-

---

* This paper was originally delivered as a lecture at the *Leonardo* "Mutamorphosis:
Challenging Arts and Sciences" conference, 8-10 November 2007, Municipal Library,
Prague.

ment that exerts inordinate social control, leading inexorably to the loss of our personal liberty. This cloud of unknowing shrouds us in anxiety and fear. This is the military/industrial complex running wild, using paranoia to control the financial and political will of elected governments. It is a paranoia challenged by the liberating telenoia of the Net, the joy of connectedness that is universally celebrated in cyberspace. None the less, who knows who will strike next, the terrorist or agents of the state? Here indeed is terror incognito.

But the real terra incognito, the final frontier of the unknown, lies not within society at large, and its culture of contingency, nor far out in the dark matter of remote galaxies, but much closer to home, within the ontological territory with which we are most intimately engaged, and of which we are most utterly ignorant, that is to say the domain of the mind. As a society, as much as we exercise our everyday awareness, we fear consciousness; we avoid exploring it, we deny its deepest dimensions, and we refute its universal connectivity and collectivity. We know nothing of where it is located, how it arises, of what it is constituted. There is a sense amongst some scientists that they do not even want to know, or dare not challenge the folk theory that mind is an epiphenomenon of the brain. Too much would be at stake if the Newtonian apple-cart were to be overturned. Think for example of the extreme denial amongst physicists in relation to the metaphysical implications of quantum mechanics. Think also of the doctrinaire rigidity of those whose fundamentalist materialism credits the brain with the creation of consciousness, who dive meat first into the mind, rather than investigating the brain as an organ of access to the field of consciousness. Think also of those hundreds of thousand, millions perhaps, of first person reports in all cultures at all times of psychic perception in all its forms, that have been routinely rejected out of hand, while psychoanalysis, whose theory Freud based on a handful of anecdotal reports, is privileged, if not as an exact science, at least with a place at the funding table.

It is actually an astrophysicist who most elegantly and succinctly provides a description of field theory, in relation to consciousness, namely Attila Grandpierre, of the Konkoly Observatory in Budapest. Grandpierre argues that

> The organisation of an organism involves fields, which are the only means to make a simultaneous tuning of the different subsystems of the organism-as-a-whole. Nature uses the olfactory fields, the acoustic fields, the electromagnetic fields and quantum vacuum fields. Fields with their ability to comprehend the whole organism are the natural basis of a global interaction between organisms and

of collective consciousness, such that electromagnetic potential fields mediate the collective field of consciousness.[1]

He offers a quantum-physical model of a multi-layered consciousness, where the layering is expressed by the subsequent subtlety of the masses of the material carriers of information. Direct, immediate action at a distance actually exists in the electromagnetic field, which is the coupling, mediator field between waves and particles. The environmental, natural and cosmic fields are determinative sources of our consciousness. The Collective Field of Consciousness is a significant physical factor of the biosphere. The morphogenetic field has an electromagnetic (EM) nature. EM fields are vacuum fields. Different basic forms of vacuum fields exist, and all kinds of fields, including the particle-mediated fields as well, when overlapping each other, seem to be in a direct resonant coupling, and form a complex, merged bio field. The vacuum model of consciousness points to the inductive generation of consciousness, and to its self-initiating nature. Individual and collective methods, as well as the experimental possibilities of a global healing and improving the consciousness field of mankind are suggested.

In general, many field theories come relatively low in the estimation of state-approved science, are unlikely to receive serious research funding, and are pushed in many cases to the margins of scientific respectability. The new organicism of May Wan Ho, the biophotonic research of Fritz-Albert Popp, the holonomic brain theory of Karl Pribram, the implicate order of David Bohm, are kept largely at arm's length by the scientific establishment. And Donna Haraway, even amongst the cognoscenti of media art, is recognised more for her Cyborg Manifesto than for her much earlier *Crystals, Fabrics, and Fields: Metaphors of Organicism in Twentieth-Century Developmental Biology*.[2]

Of considerable significance to the evolving ontology of new media art is the major shift in research focus of Tom Ray that moves from A-life to mind science. It is a research that plays a radical part in the emergence of what can be called moistmedia, that is to say the convergence of dry computational technologies and wet biological systems, since its concern is with the re-

[1] Attila Grandpierre, "The Physics of Collective Consciousness," *World Futures: The Journal of General Evolution* 48 (1997): 23-56.

[2] See Mae-Wan Ho, "Quantum Coherence and Conscious Experience," *Kybernetes* 26 (1997): 265-276; Fritz-Albert Popp and L. Beloussov, *Integrative Biophysics—Biophotonics* (Dordrecht: Kluwer Academic, 2003); Karl Pribram, *Brain and Perception: Holonomy and Structure in Figural Processing* (New York: Erlbaum, 1991); David Bohm, *Wholeness and the Implicate Order* (London: Routledge, 1980); Donna Haraway, *Crystals, Fabrics, and Fields: Metaphors of Organicism in Twentieth-Century Developmental Biology* (New Haven: Yale University Press, 1976).

evaluation of psychedelics, and by extension, the pharmacology of plants, in the understanding of mind states, and of consciousness at large. Ray was initially famous amongst new media artists and computer scientists for the creation of Tierra:

> Synthetic organisms have been created based on a computer metaphor of organic life in which CPU time is the "energy" resource and memory is the "material" resource. Memory is organised into informational patterns that exploit CPU time for self-replication. Mutation generates new forms, and evolution proceeds by natural selection as different genotypes compete for CPU time and memory space.[3]

This has been replaced by research leading to the discovery of ...

> Nineteen psychedelics [that] have each been screened against over one hundred receptors, transporters and ion channels, providing the first comprehensive view of how these compounds interact with the human receptome. Each individual psychedelic causes a unique spectrum of subjective effects. [...] We want to get to know the pharmacology of the attractors [...] to begin to map the chemical organisation of the human mind.[4]

In my view the digital moment in art has passed, it has been absorbed in practice, and assimilated by theory. A pharmacological moment is upon us, within cognitive science and beyond its borders. Only our extreme materialism, the cowardice of political expediency and cultural mind control, prevent us from exploring new worlds and participating in new realities. In the evolving technoetic culture, living in altered states of consciousness will become more frequently the norm, just as living in multiple states of body informs our living today—both in Second Life scenarios and the syncretic reality of contemporary being.

We should understand that, unlike individual, creative scientists, institutional science has always regarded art as occupying an alien, hostile territory wherein intuition is privileged over rationality, and reality is constructed without license. It warns us to avoid the extreme conditions of consciousness, to regard altered states of consciousness as constituting a threat to the orthodoxies of being, and to the stability of social norms. Indeed, even within a laboratory setting, such exploration may be treated as deviant or criminal. If we look at the history of the psychoactive drug lysergic acid di-

[3] T.S. Ray, "An Approach to the Synthesis of Life," in *Artificial Life II*, eds. C. Langton, C. Taylor, J. D. Farmer, & S. Rasmussen. Santa Fe Institute Studies in the Sciences of Complexity, vol. XI (Redwood City, CA: Addison-Wesley, 1991) 371-408.

[4] T.S. Ray, "The Chemical Architecture of the Human Mind" (2005): http://brainwaves.corante.com/archives/2005/02/05/the_chemical_architecture_of_the human_mind_by_tom_ray.php Accessed 17.8.07.

ethylamide (LSD), for example, we see a complete failure to differentiate between its medicinal, recreational and spiritual uses. The ban applied by the US government on 6 October 1966 immediately halted research on the chemistry of the brain and proscribed for decades all investigations with psychoactive materials into the nature of consciousness, as well as their use in cultural, religious and spiritual practices whose provenance spanned centuries if not millennia. The case of ayahuasca is exemplary here, in so far as it informs a continuous living culture, originating timelessly in the forests of Brazil and Colombia, which has mutated into many urban environments. As a vehicle for the exploration of mind, as a tool for the navigation of consciousness, it constitutes an exact pharmacology, a vegetal technology as precise in its operation as any Western scientific protocol. Still an illegal substance, it is only recently that the US Supreme Court found in favour of its use in specific religious ritual.

The paradox addressed here is that we occupy the most dangerous territory of mind on a daily basis, thinking that its is benign and, indeed, normal. But this simple, habitual level of thought and behaviour puts us in a state of extreme danger; in so far as the creative exploration of consciousness is concerned. Habit is the enemy that leads to the sclerosis of the self, reinforcing the passive, uncritical repetition of normative behaviours, opinions, perceptions and values. Habit is particularly the enemy of art, impeding the search for new ways of being. In art today, our computer-mediated systems are mobile, interactive and transformative; they defy docile social stability and bring evolutionary innovation to the dynamic equilibrium of living, cultural systems. In telematic culture, the multiple identity syndrome (MIS) is not pathological but affirmatively creative. We make ourselves, remix, remodel and renew both our identity and the very core of our being. We are more than ever transient and indeterminate. Eventually, with technological development, Second Life scenarios will be able more fully to accommodate the syncretism of the self.

This has not prevented technology from attempting to parallel the phenomenology of psychic agency. The telematic effect has been to distribute mind, and to vitiate its isolated autonomy, while cyberspace affords the multiplication of identity, and the telepresence of the self. For the artist to break through the extreme environment of classical science, with the hostile intentionality of its authoritarian regime, into the quantum world of (psychic) potentiality and (spiritual) becoming, both courage and vision are called for. On the other side of the world, it is in the extreme and apparently hostile environment of the forest that a technoetic approach to human transformation is exercised. This involves the technology of plants, the application of nature to the navigation of mind, through rituals that conduct us to multiple worlds without barriers, to shared realities without boundaries, and to the redefinition of what it is to be human.

At the material level, technology could provide us with another skin, another layer of energy to the body, adding to the complexity of its field. Instead of populating Second Life with (virtual) objects we would be more syncretic if we considered it as a medium for the creation of (virtual) fields, or as an extension of the biofield itself. We can see Second Life (for example) as the field in which new possibilities for living systems are being rehearsed, just as we would do best to recognise VR and Mixed Reality technologies as providing the tools to rehearse what will become actual in the evolving nanoculture. This radical change in our interaction with and construction of the material world, the almost infinite flexibility of actuation, engineering what is impossible at present, gives world-designers a huge ethical as well as aesthetic responsibility.

The life of the mind in this radically transformed world—the extremity of which it is not possible fully to comprehend at this moment—and the very status of consciousness itself will become the primary issue on the research agenda in many fields.

Ours can be described as a contingent culture. It's about chance and change, in the world, in the environment, in oneself. It is essentially syncretic. People re-invent themselves; create new relationships, new orders of time and space. Technoetics leads to serial selves, serial relationships, serial self-invention. Our culture is completely open-ended, evolving and transforming at a fast rate— just as we are, at this stage of our evolution, and just as we want it to be. Human nature, unconstrained, is essentially syncretic. Why syncretic? Just as cybernetics analogises differences between systems, so syncretism finds likeness between unlike things. If cybernetics underlies the technology of new media art, syncretism informs the psyche. Historically, syncretism has destabilised political and religious orthodoxies, reconciling and harmonising formerly discrete antagonists; its etymology derives from the coming together of opposed tribes to resist a common enemy. In contemporary culture, the enemy is habit—the uncritical repetition of behaviours, perceptions, categories, and values. Digital art is approaching the status of orthodoxy; the period of extreme speculation, invention and untrammelled creativity is in danger of giving way to academicism and commercialisation, whether in cyberspace, on the web or through the mobile. Art's 20th-century preoccupation with the body is giving way to the technoetic exploration of new territories of mind. This may involve revisiting the pathways to personal transformation and transcendence of older cultures, where the syncretism of knowledge and beliefs is explicit, as for example in Brazil. Art needs to adopt syncretic strategies to embrace emerging models of mind and matter, cyberception, living process and computational systems, moistmedia, quantum reality, the nanofield, and ecological, social and spiritual issues. This may lead to significant changes in the way we regard our own identity, our relationship to others, the nature of memory, the exploration of consciousness, and the phenomenology of time and space.

Syncretic thinking breaches boundaries and subvert protocols. Hypermedia is its telematic correlate. Thinking out of the box, searching for the extremities of perception, testing the limits of language, expression and construction, puts the artist at the edge of social and cultural norms, which in our present heavily circum-scribed society is a dangerous place to be. In religious or spiritual contexts, syncretism can mean combining from diverse sources epistemologies, rituals, psychic instruments, psychotropic plants and herbs, into new forms of sacred communion. In contemporary society, syncretism may involve combining technologies that are interactive and digital, reactive and mechanical, psychoactive and chemical, and new rituals of contemporary social networks that are mobile, locative, and online, together with a creative sensibility towards the practices of older cultures that have habitually been seen as alien, exotic and in many cases proscribed.

The real revolution in the new digital technology (which will be even more radical with the evolving nanotechnology) lies not so much that of global connectivity—person to person, mind to mind—that releases us from the constraints of time and place (great as that is), but its power to provide for the release of the self, release from the self, the fictive "unified self" that analysts and therapists relentlessly promote. The idea of making the self into one undivided whole, of finding the one true self buried deep in the unconscious can be seen as both a conjuring trick and an assault on our human nature. Ouspensky was right; we are multi-ple, made up of many selves, with access to many layers of consciousness. Rather than needing to go deep into ones self, we need to reach out to the many selves that our innate creativity craves. This is where the revolution in consciousness lies; in our ability to be many selves, to be telematically in many places at the same time, our digital and post-biological self-creation leading to many personas, many aspects of what we each can be. In short, the 21st-century self is generative. This is of course the appeal of Second Life, as it is to the many narratives and games of genera-tive identity, shape-shifting, and transformative personality that new media art has created.

It was syncretic thought that led John Whiteside Parsons—one of the early pioneers of rocket science—to claim that we should no longer see ourselves as creatures chained to the earth but as beings capable of exploring the universe, while at the same time believing that unseen metaphysical worlds existed that could be explored with the right knowledge. He saw no contradiction between his scientific and magical pursuits: before each rocket test launch, Parsons would ritually invoke the god Pan.[5] Frank Malina (whose life and work we are celebrating in this conference), Ed Forman and Parsons together formed the country's first governmental rocket group. Malina's syncretism was later expressed in his practice as a visionary techno-artist, scientist and cultural integrationist; it was my privilege to have known him at this part of his career. Parsons experimented extensively with the occult, becoming a key figure in Aleister Crowley's Ordo Templi Orientis, in Los Angeles in the 1930s. Contrary to those who saw magic and science as inherently contradictory, to Parsons they were complementary, two sides of the same coin. A close friend of Crowley was the Portuguese poet Fernando Pessoa, a writer deeply involved with altered states of consciousness and reliant upon the world of the spirits.

Ricardo Reis, Alvaro dos Campos, Alberto Caeiro, and Bernardo Soares are writers whose place in Portuguese letters are assured. They are in fact heteronyms of Fernando Pessoa, with their own individual histories, appearances, emotional qualities, philosophies, and style of writing: they are not pseudonyms. Were Pessoa to be active today, they would probably be wholly differentiated avatars, artistically and politically active in Second Life. As John Gray has pointed out, "Fernando Pessoa invented at least 72 fictive identities. These jostling aliases express his belief that the individual subject—the core of European thought—is an illusion."[6] Therein lies Pessoa's significance today. He well understood the notion of the distributed self, that we are each many selves. Pessoa left a trunk containing over 25,000 items: poems, letters, journals—writings on philosophy, sociology, history, literary criticism, plays, treatises on astrology, observations on the occult, esoterica of many kinds—written by dozens of heteronyms. Pessoa's psychological and literary prescience, and the breadth and complexity of his interests, anticipated life in our hypertextual world of the Web, where the fluidity of associative links and genres, and the instability, variability and transformation of identities and personas is one of its

---

[5] George Pendle, *Strange Angel: The Otherworldly Life of Rocket Scientist John Whiteside Parsons* (New York: Harcourt, 2005).

[6] John Gray, "Assault on Authorship," *New Statesman* (28 May 2007).

greatest appeals and challenges. We can only imagine what his (dis)embodied syncretism might have brought to the telematic embrace. Through his exploration of consciousness, he developed occult skills and paranormal powers, including spiritualist mediumship, telepathy, and especially his development of "etheric vision":

> There are moments when I have sudden flashes of "etheric vision" and can see certain people's "magnetic auras" and especially my own, reflected in the mirror, and radiating from my hands in the dark. In one of my best moments of etheric vision [...] I saw someone's ribs through his coat and skin [...]. My "astral vision" is still very basic, but sometimes, at night, I close my eyes and see a swift succession of small and sharply defined pictures [...]. I see strange shapes, designs, symbolic signs, numbers [...].[7]

The challenge to our syncretic model of thought and action in the context of creativity is to untie the Newtonian knot that binds our perception, and seek always to put subject before object, process before system, behaviour before form, intuition before reason, mind before matter.

In order to meet the needs of the culture of contingency, and properly to accommodate and sustain the generative Self, our agenda should seek to amplify thought, share consciousness, seed structures, make metaphors, and construct identities. A truly technoetic and syncretic art will embrace concepts of biophysics: coherence, macroscopic quantum states, long-range interactions, non-linearity, self-organisation and self-regulation, communication networks, field models, interconnectedness, non-locality, and the inclusion of consciousness.

By way of conclusion, or overture if you have not previously considered the issues I have briefly raised here, I leave you with a map (below) of the forces and fields which contribute, as I see it, to the evolving syncretic reality in which we live.

---

[7] Fernando Pessoa, *The Selected Prose of Fernando Pessoa*, trans. by Richard Zenith (New York: Grove Press, 2001).

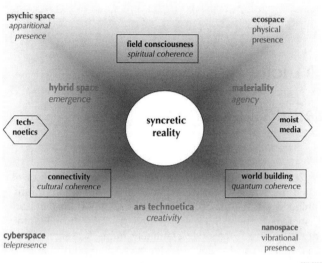

Niall Lucy

Poetry & Deconstruction

At the 2007 APEC summit in Sydney, where the leaders of nations belonging to the Asia-Pacific economic co-operation forum met, something weird happened. With so many important dignitaries on hand, including the US President and his 650-strong entourage, security in Sydney was understandably tight. A steel-and-concrete barricade stretching for several kilometres along both sides of central city streets marked the borders of a restricted zone extending from the visitors' hotels to the summit venue, forcing local traffic to be re-routed. Sydneysiders were given a public holiday and encouraged to get out of town, presumably to make it all the easier for police and security personnel, armed to the teeth with hi-tech weapons and telecommunications devices, to spot foreign terrorists and stay-at-home domestic troublemakers alike. Protest rallies calling for reduced greenhouse gas emissions, or for Australia and the US to pull out of Iraq, were subject to strict state control, and demonstrators with prior convictions were arrested on sight. Shots of security preparations in the city and at Sydney airport, featuring police in riot gear and armoured vehicles fitted with crowd-busting water canons, were prominent in the national media for days leading up to the summit.

Then, suddenly, in a comedic moment of deconstruction, the unity of all this spectacular apparatus of security (reputedly costing $250 million) was rent asunder. A group of comedians from Australian TV show *The Chaser's War on Everything*, disguised as Canadian APEC officials, drove a motorcade of three black limousines and a motorcycle escort through the fenced-off streets of Sydney's central business district, using false ID cards stamped with "joke" to clear several checkpoints along the way, before finally being intercepted ten metres outside the entrance to the

---

* This piece is taken from my forthcoming introduction to John Kinsella's *Derrida Poems*.

Intercontinental Hotel where the US contingent was staying. Adding to the already carnivalesque nature of the scene, one of the group (Chas Licciardello) was dressed up to look like Osama bin Laden. He is reported to have stepped from a limousine and said to police, indignantly, "I am a world leader. Why haven't I been invited to APEC too?"

Footage of the incident (taken by the comedy show's film crew) was quickly posted on YouTube and televised around the world, no doubt to the amusement of many. But Australian authorities failed to see the funny side and charged the comedians with offences under newly legislated national security laws, which carry a maximum penalty of six months in jail. As Sydney's police chief sternly put it: the group had placed themselves and others in serious danger, because snipers were positioned all over the city and the slightest miscommunication among security forces could have seen things go horribly wrong!

Predictably humourless and admonishing, the response of the police chief and other state officials (along with state advocates, as they might be called, such as conservative media commentators) can be said not to have *read* this event at all. Official representations of the event took it to be saturated with a single meaning that bordered on sedition and justified the state in castigating the comedians for having disrespected its authority. Above all, what had to be repelled was any suggestion that the comedians' actions might have exposed the elaborate security measures in Sydney as an inevitably empty and groundless *spectacle* of state control; no more than an *exhibition* of totalising authority manufactured from simulacra designed to conceal a lack of presence. How else to account for the consummate ease by which the restricted zone was infiltrated? How else to interpret the event except as farce ... or, more menacingly, as a revelation of just how close civilians might have come, and might always be, to being shot dead by the state in the name of national security if not also (perversely) in the name of democracy?

Nothing undermines the authority of the state, let alone the authority of authority, more so than too much reading. That's why Australian authorities had no choice but to reproach *The Chaser* crew for refusing the solemn univocity of security arrangements at the APEC summit, by reading the meaning and purpose of those arrangements against the interests of the state and demonstrating that their univocity depended on the suppression of other possible interpretations that could be made of them and other possible uses to which they might be put. In this way it is sometimes seditious to crack a joke, even if the joke's effects (as perhaps in the case of *The Chaser* episode) cannot be said to have been consciously intended or fully calculated in advance. A joke, then, can reveal that even the sanctity of a so-called intended meaning is not impervious to ridicule, showing that what anything is said to mean is irreducible to a restricted zone of proper interpretations and legitimate truths. The authority of such a zone, together with the authority of a notion of the proper and of the very idea of authority itself, depends on putting all jokes aside.

But by joking here I don't mean (on the contrary) the production of a humorous effect that is necessarily universal, as if it were possible to contemplate a form of comedy that crossed all cultural, national, historical, linguistic and other borders. I mean rather, as we say in Australia, *taking the piss*. To do so is to mock authority, poking fun especially at its self-importance and always—always—with a straight face. You take the piss, in other words, when you create a *pharmakon* effect or a double reading, because for a split second at least the impassive tone and demeanour of your delivery make it undecidable as to whether your intentions are serious or ironic. Piss-taking—as in the case of *The Chaser* crew's simulated performance of a proper APEC group seeming to act in accordance with appropriate rules and procedures, such as those pertaining to the proper image, speed and motion of a cortege—is all about appearing to play by the rules of one language game while in fact playing by the rules of another. Piss-taking depends on refusing to be interpellated as the obedient subject of a discourse, who would otherwise comply with the expectations of a role assigned to him or her by a figure, a structure, an institution or some other instance of authority.

The Fool in *King Lear* is an exemplar of the type, but the piss-taker as social critic (in a progressively disruptive, Nietzschean fashion) is perhaps more comfortably aligned, however marginally, with a modernity associated with the Enlightenment. To the extent that the Enlightenment stands for the triumph of *logos* over *mythos*, though, piss-taking is frowned upon by official discourse. The secular, scientific authority of rational thought (substituting for the theocratic authority of the monarchy and the aristocracy) is intolerant of the dissidence of fools.

Hence the piss-taking prankster is fated to be marginalised from within a metaphysics that takes itself all too seriously. Such a figure at least is destined to be "controversial," for daring to confront the Enlightenment with the vanity of its self-importance. Tonally, as it were, the droning seriousness of Kant is deadening to the soul; and for the same reason I can't read Heidegger for long (assuming the jokes haven't been lost in translation) without reaching for my car keys or the remote control. For all that the Enlightenment has given us the possibility of democracy and the promise of a better future to come, for which there is no question a better future to come, for which there is no question that we should be eternally grateful, sometimes you can't help yourself from wanting the piss to be taken out of everything—concepts, discourses, institutions—that has been reified to an all but mythological level of gravitas commanding nothing but aloof respect.

It is precisely for this reason that deconstruction, for example, which takes the piss out of metaphysics, has never quite been accorded official status by the institution of philosophy (or state philosophy as it might be called, following Deleuze and Guattari); certainly not in the English-speaking West, where the Intercontinental Hotel of authority is reserved more or less exclusively for the delegates of the analytic tradition. The more Derrida wrote, the more his writing caused offence to philosophy's self-representation as a non-metaphorical system in pursuit of transcendental signifieds. Ideally, philosophy goes looking for truths that are already there, waiting to be translated into language; and the more Derrida's writing failed to revere this ideal, by taking the piss out of it, the more his writing came to be dismissed as playfully specious rather than seriously philosophical. The more it came to be seen as a species of poetry, in other words, albeit without it being seen at the same time that all poetry takes the piss out of language.

Poetry scoffs at the presumption that good sense is a product of plain language use, based on the idea that truth is prior to and independent of its representations. Through unadorned expression, then, *logos* overcomes the dangerous supplementarity of *mythos*. But by extending free passage to others and opening itself to interpretation, every poem mocks the vanity of this presumption that underlies the possibility of a purely referential language; hence the function of the institution of literary criticism is to restrict the in-principle limitless interpretability of poetic texts to a zone of proper meanings, protected by a barricade of mystifying professional-esoteric terminology and knowledge subject to radical reappraisal from time to time. Taking a different view, what Derrida can be said to have done—every word he wrote—is reducible to this subversive insight: what is true of poetic texts is true of textuality in general. If this were not so—if indeed every text did have an ineluctable core meaning—then someone would have figured out the meaning of *Hamlet* a long time ago, and that would have been that.

Hamlet continues to surprise because it continues to be read in different ways, and not always as an example of literature. In *Specters of Marx*, for instance, Derrida reads it not as an illustration of the pop-psychological consequences of procrastination, but for what it has to say politically and philosophically about the spectral nature of democracy-to-come. Such a reading both defies the institutional authority of literary criticism, which values the play for its aesthetic and morally educative qualities, while refusing to respect the proper objects and methods of political philosophy. Derrida reads *Hamlet*, in a word, as text—in excess of its canonical status as a literary masterwork and therefore against the interests of authority vested in established (if not establishment) notions of literature, philosophy and politics.

A disrespect for genre—the mark perhaps of a deconstructive, as distinct from a straightforwardly critical, reading—is a feature too, I think, of John Kinsella's work, extending across poetry, essays, fiction and other kinds of writing. Hilariously—at least to this Australian—one of Kinsella's books is called *Genre* (marketed all too predictably in the publishing world as a novel), a text which defies generic classification while imitating just about every genre under the sun. As a piss-take of the literature department's and the publishing industry's careful attempts to make sense of writing-in-general, by assigning to every text a secure place in the periodic table of writings-in-particular, it is also (as McKenzie Wark notes) part of Kinsella's "ongoing experiment of becoming a writer."[1] This experiment—an extravagant essay in border crossing, as it were—is less an act of transgression, requiring the conscious renunciation of a limit, than an affirmation of enjambment. Being John Kinsella is all about running on, spilling over, re-territorialising. Again, as Wark puts it:

> Whether conceived as a hierarchy, from literature to kitsch, or as layered from central to peripheral traditions, writing is one of the most territorialised of the arts. But as the vectors of communication change, so too can the practices of writing and reading. The local can go global without depending on the intermediate step in the hierarchy of aesthetic territories—the nation. But as a paradoxical result, need not renounce the national in order to escape it.[2]

Kinsella's status as a national—an "Australian"—poet is something he neither embraces nor shuns; nor should his "Australianness" be thought to be translatable into other national contexts, as if the reception to his poetry downunder could be superimposed elsewhere. Lauded overseas for the greatness of his lyric poetry by Harold Bloom and for the greatness of his experimental poetry by Marjorie Perloff, Kinsella's border crossings (and not only between supposedly divergent poetic traditions, as if there were some com-

---

[1] Mckenzie Wark, "Generator: Thinking Through John Kinsella's *Genre*" in *Fairly Obsessive: Essays on the Works of John Kinsella*, eds. Rod Mengham and Glen Phillips (Fremantle: Fremantle Arts Centre Press, 2000) 256.
[2] Wark, "Generator," 271.

pelling reason to choose between the Metaphysicals and the Romantics) make him a scandalous figure in the world of Australian letters, where there are those who refer to him dismissively as a big-time operator on the poetry business scene. What most seems to rankle with Australian critics (aside, perhaps, from petty resentment) is that Kinsella so conspicuously *works* at being a poet— through his national and international academic appointments and contacts, his media interviews, his publishing and editorial ventures, his appearances at conferences, festivals and poetry readings—that his poems are tainted with the suggestion of being careerist rather than sincere. "Somehow," as Sydney University academic Ivor Indyk wrote, in a now notorious review of Kinsella's *Poems 1980-1994* for the influential *Australian Book Review*, "his energy is so overwhelming that it makes the quality of his poetry seem like a secondary consideration."[3] More recently, in a sneering review of Kinsella's *Fast, Loose Beginnings: A Memoir of Intoxications* for the liberal daily, *The Sydney Morning Herald*, poet and University of Queensland academic Jaya Savige complained that Kinsella "appears drunk on the éclat of luminous literary acquaintance" while simultaneously (and hypocritically, it is implied) cultivating his status as an outsider.[4] Further afield, meanwhile, no less a luminous literary authority than Harold Bloom has said of Kinsella that "if there still be, this late, a 'pure' poet, it would be him, free of ideologies and of any histories that are not personal"— and whatever *that* (in a post-Derridean /Deleuzian/Foucauldian context) might mean, it is clearly intended as praise of an unambiguously high order.[5]

Kinsella's contradictions—he is an Australian who is also a cosmopolitan; an Antipodean *and* a Cambridge poet; a lyricist *and* an experimentalist; a "pure" poet *and* a publicity seeker; an ex-junkie who is now a vegan; a country boy who knows his way around many of the world's great cities; a critic of the academy who enjoys the institutional and other benefits of professorial residencies at Cambridge and the University of Western Australia, having previously held a chair at Kenyon College in the United States—loom large in most discussions of his work, fanning the controversy that surrounds both "it" and the poet "himself." The assumption seems to be that the rest of us are fully unified sub-

---

[3] Ivor Indyk, "Kinsella's Hallmarks," *Australian Book Review* (July 1997): http://home.vicnet.net.au/~abr/July97/indyk.html

[4] Jaya Savige, "[Rev. of] *Fast, Loose Beginnings: A Memoir of Intoxications*," *Sydney Morning Herald*, 21 August 2006: http://www.smh.com.au/news/book-reviews/fast-loose-beginnings-a-memoir-of-intoxications/2006/08/21/1156012451 866. html

[5] Harold Bloom, "Introduction" in John Kinsella, *Peripheral Light: Selected New Poems* (Fremantle: Fremantle Arts Centre Press, 2003) xxii.

jects, our innermost selves remaining constant around the clock. In compliance with the metaphysics of moderation we consign our becoming to all manner of discursive scrutiny and regulation, as we know from *Discipline and Punish* and other works by Foucault, arresting difference in the bargain. As we know from Derrida, though, a certain idea of writing—as dissemination, as enjambment—takes the piss out of both the sovereign subject and of subjectivity "itself," along with the idea that meaning is determined by the elemental properties of a text. Deconstruction goes beyond structuralism, then, both philosophically and in its affrontery (albeit without renouncing structuralism), by dissociating meaning not only from authorial subjectivity, but from the authority of presence in all its conceptual, historical, institutional, political and other forms. Once the signifier-signified relationship is understood as *radically* arbitrary and indeterminate, it is no longer possible to read a text according to the structuralist ideal—as a simultaneous system of internal relations. Simultaneity—the myth of a reading that would describe the operations of the various parts of a text at once, such that the text would be present in its totality—precludes, after all, any consideration of whatever does not conform to it. Whatever "cannot be spread out into the simultaneity of a form," as Derrida put it a long time ago, structuralism finds "intolerable"; and since this is true as well of metaphysics generally, structuralism cannot be confined to a movement or a method associated with the likes of Saussure and Lévi-Strauss.[6] This is why, although structuralists may be good at analysing the formal properties of a joke, it has never occurred to them to crack a few jokes of their own: the metaphysics of authority depends on putting all jokes aside.

Some would say Kinsella was attracted to the *danger* of being attracted to Derrida, consciously or otherwise courting excommunication from the poetry world for associating with a figure who is still more vilified than vindicated in literary circles (outside the academy certainly) worldwide. Others might point even less charitably to Derrida's *notoriety* as the shiny object of Kinsella's desire, re-writing their friendship as a calculated move in the game of managing a reputation for defiance on the poet's part. Within and beyond the academy, such crude psychological speculation remains the order of the day—no less for professional criticism and philosophy than for popular media discourses. After Derrida, then, and after Foucault and Deleuze and Lyotard and Barthes and Baudrillard and all the rest, the motorcade of metaphysics continues to run its

---

[6] Jacques Derrida, "Force and Signification" in *Writing and Difference*, trans. Alan Bass (London: Routledge & Kegan Paul, 1978) 25.

course, those seeking to disrupt it having been overcome for now by the official and unofficial security forces of a new world order of seriousness in the face of imminent terrorist attacks. In this context, nothing serves the interests of metaphysics—let alone the West's interest in oil—better than a prosaic imagination.

That's what I think the poems in this collection are "about," although not in any kind of thematic sense. What I think attracts Kinsella to Derrida's writing is not so much the shock value (though of course he is aware of this effect) as the *mundanity* of deconstruction, which takes a certain kind of imagination—a poetic or aesthetic imagination—to respond to without fear or favour, or without prejudice of a certain kind. How could a statement such as Derrida's now notorious claim in the *Grammatology*, that "there is nothing outside of the text," be read by a poet, except as a perfectly unextraordinary thing to think or say—despite many real-life poets' denial that Derrida wrote anything worth reading at all?[7] What does it tell us about the world and what it may be necessary to change, when the positions of soft-hearted liberals and hard-line conservatives alike are as one in condemning deconstruction for disrespecting the authority of tradition, Western values and standards of truth? When liberals *and* conservatives are arm-in-arm opposed to the dangerous "relativism" of deconstruction, what does this tell us about deconstruction?

One of the ways in which the poems here can be seen to respond to such a question is simply by taking that question seriously, which is to say by taking deconstruction seriously. Which is to say, by not taking deconstruction *too* seriously. Take the following fragment from "The Echidna and Hedgehog bear only Superficial Resemblances":

> birdsnoutducklike
> all mammary glands
> and egg drop
> and body hair
> mammal inter reptilian
> but not a metamorphosis,
> which is so convenient
> for the human condition,
> as lucrative as television

This is not what the writing of a professional philosopher, a sociologist or a literary critic looks like, though it does tolerate a certain similarity to the writing of my ten-year-old son. Children write "po-

7 Jacques Derrida, *Of Grammatology*, trans. Gayatri Chakravorty Spivak (Baltimore: Johns Hopkins University Press, 1976) 158.

etically," in other words, before they learn how to write prose. They assemble words haphazardly, "creatively," on a page or screen, seemingly unencumbered by the need to stretch each line of type or script to fit a standard margin width. They create, or simply form, weird new "words" out of combinations of existing words and syllables—*birdsnoutducklike*—long before learning to recognise these as *portmanteau* words, like "actuvirtuality" or "phonocentrism." They describe things elliptically, and almost exclusively through a mixture of parataxis, conjunction and enjambment: "all mammary glands/and egg drop/and body hair/mammal inter reptilian." In this way poetry—or the creative force of childrens' language use—is precisely what has to be unlearned in order to learn to write prose. Prose (when it isn't fiction) is poetry stripped of its creative force, and we learn to write it acceptably only by forgetting that, before we learned to write "properly," we played with language in the absence of any pressure to conform to the referential imperative of professional nonfiction, as if writing on the basis of a mundane truth: *there is no outside of the text*. Between poetry and prose, then, there are only superficial resemblances, though we are said to write prose well (rather than just adequately) by virtue of a certain metamorphosis with poetry, whenever our writing incorporates a trope, a striking turn of phrase or some other prosodic feature deployed to good effect. Poetic devices, but not quite poetry as such, can lead therefore to lucrative professional and cultural, if not also financial, rewards, for those judged to control their otherwise chaotic—pre-prosaic—potential.

This is what Wark means when he calls writing one of the most territorialised of the arts. So we have poets, and we give them a licence to write "poetically" or aesthetically (according to a certain idea of literature), relegating poetry to a "special" kind of writing and in the process delimiting what it can be used to do. And so we have critics, and we give them the authority not only to determine what counts as poetry but also to police its borders. And so we have institutions, and we give them the authority to sanction and patrol the limits of what counts as poetry. And so we have a publishing industry, and we give it the authority to market poetry to readers. In all of this what we don't have is an idea of writing in general ... and so we have philosophers, and we give them the authority to be philosophical by virtue of showing us the extent of their mastery over the irruptive, aleatory, figural and other undesirable effects of language. Which is to say, of poetry. And so we have historians, and we give them the authority to tell us what history means ... and so on.

Poetry comes before prose, which is what this territorialising system is designed to suppress. And because poetry comes before prose, Derrida sometimes delighted in taking the piss out of the idea of a well formatted page (as the image of a well formulated argument). Think, for instance, of *Dissemination* and *Glas*. In the "poetic" episodes of some of his work, Derrida's writing is conspicuous in quite literal ways (as if in reaction to the po-faced seriousness of the *Grammatology*), inviting readers to engage with it outside the constraints of standard sense-making protocols. This—turning readers into active participants in the production of meanings by opening the possibility of doing philosophy differently and doing different things with it—raised the ire of straight-laced philosophers, who could not but look on any disruption to the solidified territorialisation of writing as a professional threat. Their ungracious indignation stooped to its lowest point in the early 1990s, when some Cambridge dons (including a few from Kinsella's own Churchill College, though this was before his time there) tried to block Cambridge's offer of an honourary doctorate to Derrida for services to philosophy.[8] Deconstruction it seemed was no laughing matter, and the best way of putting a stop to its profanities was to try to have Derrida, in effect, de-registered! And so now all these years later another Cambridge don—albeit from the antipodes, at the limits of Western civilisation—has written a book of poems, in effect, "for" Derrida if not quite about him. In the context of what ought to be Cambridge's shame, the ethics of this gesture should not go unnoticed.

---

[8] See Niall Lucy, *Debating Derrida* (Melbourne: Melbourne University Press, 1995) for the details.

Christina Ljungberg

Mapping Fluid Spaces:
Semiotic Bodies & Cyberart

As new technologies generate new technosocial spaces, new strategies of orientation become necessary. This is a development that has caught the attention of contemporary artists who have been investigating the spaces created by new and sophisticated technologies—the Internet, GPS, WLAN, international databanks, RFID object space, smart architecture / fluid architecture, etc. These so-called "anthropo-technical" spaces are radically changing not only our relationships with the life-world but also the way we orient ourselves in space. How do we experience these spaces that are characterised by an instantaneous and dynamic relationship between humans and technology? And how can we locate ourselves in a world that is increasingly IT-dominated and therefore fluid, instantaneous and consistently interacting? What new systems of orientation are required to explore these spaces that have been scientifically but not yet philosophically investigated, as these mappings do not only concern novel kinds of spatial awareness?

These and similar questions have recently been insistently interrogated by digital artists who even more specifically attempt to map the new forms of human positions and positioning produced by our active and continuous interchanges in realtime. This implies nothing less than new modes of subjectivity. Although maps have to some extent always fulfilled these functions, what is different today are the technologies at our disposal which not only generate new dynamic spaces but also *demand* the development of new mapping strategies allowing for both improvisational and subjective positioning in constant negotiations for space. I would go even further and suggest that the works by these artists imply that the subject-object framework be relinquished for that of an implicated agent and an expansive field in which the agency of any identifiable presence is intertwined with other agencies. From this follows further that the sensorial experience of such a field or space becomes a function of the way the agent relates to the form of mapping employed.

Locating the subject has always been one of the prime functions of maps—it is interesting to follow how, at the time of geographical expansion, cartographic writing developed when writers such as Rabelais, Montaigne and Cervantes sought to "map out" their worlds for their readers by appropriating the worlds they were navigating through discourse and space. As maps were plotted a new self emerged which was partly defined by the relationship of the self to space; a subject that had to develop new strategies to deal with the Cartesian space that Western maps embody, making him or her an omniscient spectator of the projected space that maps represented as objects of art, science and technology. What is different today are the technologies at our and therefore also at the disposal of artists, because not only do these technologies generate new dynamic spaces, they even *demand* the development of new mapping strategies.

This field could then be called an "agential space," as suggested by Vincent Colapietro, and which he sees as a space in which agents are at once caught up transcending their immediate control and implicated in the effective exercise of their somatic, social agency.[1] It involves improvisational and variable perspectives and positions of agents involved in incessant interpretation and recontextualisation. Pragmatic-semiotic research and cyberart join hands here as such an approach would seem to carry the potential not only for theorising different fields of research but also for a fruitful dialogue among cultural theory, technicity, and digital art, which I will discuss examining the works by digital artists Stelarc, Rejane Cantoni and Daniela Kutschat.

New Spaces

"Agential space," then, designates the field in which the agency of any identifiable presence is intertwined with other agencies. In other words, these agents or presences are such situated and embodied forces that the exercise of agency is best understood in terms of introducing disturbances into this field, or tracing these intersecting force patterns. The notion of "agential space" seems all the more relevant in view of the extent to which new technologies increasingly influence our lives. As Nigel Thrift puts it,

---

[1] Vincent Colapietro, personal communication 21 February 2007.

We have to look at how, as a result of the intervention of software and new forms of address, these background time-spaces are changing their character, producing novel kinds of behaviours that would not have been possible before and new types of objects which presage more active environments.[2]

In other words, the instantaneous positioning relationship that these new technologies produce are based on an *Umwelt* of information, which releases humans into a coordinate system of (re-) active realtime. The new strategies and grammars of orientation that such coordinate systems demand have already been analysed from the perspectives of the natural and technological sciences. The Humanities have, however, not yet taken full account of what this development implies, in particular the extent to which it has created a need to redefine anthropological conditions and practices.

What Thrift attempts to do is to map the human environment, "to capture the outlines of a world just coming into existence, one which is based on continuous calculation at each and every point along each and every line of movement."[3] New grammars of orientation demand new forms of mapping. What is characteristic for the ongoing technological revolution, however, is the informatisation of space and a direct embedding of the representation in the spatial structure and in the spatialising technologies themselves.

Of prime interest here is therefore the medial spaces and complex practices of orientation developing against the background of this IT-based folding together of space—map—human. But how can such fluid spaces be mapped? And what would the maps and the mapping of this new space look like? I would argue that the focus would have to shift to the relationship between agent(s) and map. Following Ingold and others, I will argue that, rather than the often-used metaphor of the map as network, these new maps would have to be meshworks.[4] In the sense intended here, meshes are formed by intervowen lines articulating heterogeneous components which produce dynamic diagrams interacting so as to avoid collisions but yet affording growth and movement (cf. de Certeau's "wandering lines"). In other words, they are processes involving diagrammatic thought of illimitable scope rather than closed systems of finite objects. Such a pragmatic approach implicates a dialogic and communicative self immersed in incessant recontextualisation and, therefore, involves mappings of the intermeshing

[2] Nigel Thrift, "Movement-Space: The Changing Domain of Thinking Resulting from the Development of New Kinds of Spatial Awareness," *Theory of Culture and Society* 4 (November 2004): 583.

[3] Thrift, "Movement-Space," 583.

[4] Cf. Tim Ingold, *The Perception of the Environment* (London: Routledge, 2000).

between agents ceaselessly participating in and responding to their environments.

What kind of maps?

Let me therefore start by defining a map from a semiotic perspective. A map is a diagram, the graphic register of correspondence between two spaces that relationally represents its object. It is this relational quality that provides diagrams with the claim to more or less objectively represent "reality" that has become discounted in other forms of representation today. I would argue that what makes the diagram such a useful figuration is that

* diagrams are relatively independent to their objects: the relationship between the objects exists independent of the map, and can be independently located and calculated.
* diagrams are abstracted to a certain criteria of relevance that can be generalised.
* diagrams represent both intelligible and sensible relations: they do not need to represent something that exists but can also be a model for the production of something new, e.g. a blue-print of an architect's drawing for the construction of a house.

This is what accounts for the creative potential of diagrams: since they allow experimenting on, both on paper, on screen or in our minds, this very feature makes them excellent tools for outlining both thought and action. It makes them indispensable for formal reasoning: according to Charles Sanders Peirce, diagrammatic reasoning is fundamental to our thought processes. The diagram is a complex iconic sign affording—indeed, inviting—such possibilities of manipulation and transformation as it "suppresses a quantity of details, and so allows the mind more easily to think of its important features."[5]

But what is particular with diagrams such as maps is their strong indexical properties, which is what I would argue accounts for their dynamism: diagrams presuppose, even demand interaction. This lies in the indexicality of the diagram / map as a visual sign. Even though the diagram is iconic, it is, as a visual sign, always "embodied in some particular materiality or particular form, or as instance of an iconic representation."[6] A diagram always refers

[5] Charles Sanders Peirce, *Collected Papers*, eds. Charles Hartshorne, Paul Weiss and Arthur Burks (Cambridge, MA: Harvard University Press, 1974 [1931-58]): 2.282.

[6] Cf. Lucia Santaella, *Matrizes da linguagem e pensamento* (Sao Paulo: Iluminuras, 2001).

to something—even more so, it calls our attention to the object it refers to and to the formal similarity between these relations.

This becomes vital in map reading. Since the most important function of maps is their interaction with their users, these therefore become part and parcel of the map action—because users must locate themselves within the map to engage with it in order to orientate themselves not only within the map but in the "real" or imaginary space it represents. With map reading, "I am here" becomes "I am there"—a strange fusion of a deictic gesture that points *from* the body to the map and at the same time to itself: the diagram or map user, as a body positioned in space, is therefore an essential part of it. Indexicality becomes the condition for the possibility of operating a map. Because maps demand an active user to function, their bird's-eye or vertical orthogonal view was once made for those who needed an overview to survey their commercial enterprises or lands. That is what makes modern maps offsprings of modernity and embodying the idea of the sovereign subject—not only is the map made from the viewpoint of a "celestial eye," but in order to use the map, the user *must* depart from an "all-seeing" perspective or position, mentally taking in—seizing—the environment from his or her point of view.[7] This development focused on maps as objects and products instead of processes of mapping: the convention of perspective made the late Medieval and Renaissance spectator and mapmaker into "a totalising eye," seeing the world as a *tableau* and plan.[8]

The modern map can thus be seen as the epitome of Cartesian subjectivity. Maps were once instrumental for the development of the Cartesian concepts of time and space[9] and it might well be that they will be essential for developing the new sense of space and time instigated by our new technologies. In contrast to earlier measurements of space that were taken at a specific point in time, calculated and transferred into a static map, our IT-based space today is, as Nigel Thrift reminds us, "based on continuous calculation at each and every point along each and every line of movement."[10] But, as he points out, at the same time these new understandings of space and time are characterised by a sense as being "more plastic, constantly mobile and dynamic."

---

[7]   Michel de Certeau, *The Practice of Everyday Life* (Berkeley: University of California Press, 1984) 92.

[8]   Certeau, *The Practice of Everyday Life*, 92.

[9]   Cf. Jeremy Black, *Maps and History* (London: Reaktion, 1997) 7.

[10]   Thrift, "Movement-Space," 583.

Mapping space

How can this space be mapped? What features of our present mapping practices can be applied to these new evolving "qualculative" fields?[11] These are fields which, as he points out,

> demands certain kinds of perceptual labour which involves forms of reflexivity that positions the subject as an instrument for seeing, rather than as an observer, in which a number of the mechanisms that we take for granted have been integrated into larger systems or into specialised feedback processes. Increasingly agents do not encounter finished, preexisting objects but rather "clearings" that disclose opportunities to intervene in the flow.[12]

However new, these apprehensions of space and time are still based on the mathematical calculations without which our virtual worlds would be unthinkable. They depend on a "fine grid of calculation," which is what makes these new capacities at all possible. Such a grid must necessarily be some kind of diagram, which not only embodies the multiple calculations which produced it but which indeed has the possibility to produce new senses of spatial— and temporal—knowledge. It must necessarily also be performative, since it generates new space relative to it, which would mean that, far from being a static and finite object, it should open up new spatial possibilities and potential. Mapping becomes a question of perspectives and positions of agents who are implicated in these spaces and a practice allowing for both improvisational and subjective positioning in continuous negotiations for space.

These kinds of processes could be seen as a modern anthropotechnical version of the archaic practice of "wayfaring," which produced sketch maps of travels and voyages from lines. Comparing the function and form of the lines on a sketch maps with those of cartographic maps, the anthropologist Tim Ingold argues that, whereas the sketch map consists of lines drawn *along* a surface, "scientific" or modern cartographic maps go *across*, cutting through the ocean following the course plotted by the navigator.[13] Once arrived (although preserved in a logbook), the "ruled" line can be rubbed out. The "sketched" line, however, is narrative: it is a gesture drawn in a close context to its referent and thus highly indexical as it is made up of stories of comings and goings.

These highly indexicalised maps disappeared with the development of modern cartography, which relied on the subject-object relation to the environment. That relationship was presupposed by

---

[11] Thrift, "Movement-Space," 592.

[12] Thrift, "Movement-Space," 593.

[13] Ingold, *The Perception of the Environment*, 56; 230.

Cartesian subjectivity, which made the user of the map an omniscient spectator. Such a dualist approach to the world is precisely what these new technologies now seem to challenge by evoking new modes of agency as involvement in social sets of practices. Moreover, these new modes replace the subject-object relation with that of the map user as a socially situated agent improvising in an expansive field. This field is crisscrossed with patterns of other agencies and in which agents as such are inescapably implicated in the lives and activities of other agents, orienting her or himself along the lines of the meshwork formed by the interaction between her or him and the environment. These agents are therefore participants, responding, reacting and interacting to and with other agents as well as to the environment, creatively transforming and transfiguring it. Moreover, the agents'–our–relationship to themselves or to ourselves is always made more complex by our relationship to others. That is why we are always situated and embodied forces whose exercise of agency is best understood in terms of introducing disturbances into a particular space or of tracing the complex, consistently emerging patterns of intertwining forces as an ongoing dialogue between us and our *Umwelt*.

Mapping fluid spaces
This development has caught the attention of artists who have always been at the forefront of technosocial developments. Those working in digital media in particular have been insistently interrogating the consequences and the potential of such intermeshing processes. Seizing the opportunity to both thematise and explore what these new technosocial environments *mean* and what positions and perspectives they create, artists have consistently been blurring and eroding the boundaries between subject and object by mapping their bodies into cyberspace as an expansive and dynamic field, positioning themselves and others as responsive agents. Such transmediality shifts the attention from the individual body to complex human–technology interfaces within collective infrastructures. As Johannes Birringer points out, the resulting interactivity indicates "a new understanding of environments of relations / responsibility and a relational aesthetics based on interhuman exchange or physical interaction as well as a new technological kinesthetics."[14]

---

[14] Johannes Birringer, "Interacting: Performance & Transmediality," *Monologues: Theatre, Performance, Subjectivity*, ed. Clare Wallace (Prague: Litteraria Pragensia, 2006) 300.

One of the first to engage with this kind of feedback system and cybernetic loops was the Australian performance artist Stelarc. Stelarc's project for the past twenty years has been to try to redesign the body by the means of various prostheses in order to overcome the body's shortcomings in an increasingly technosocial environment. As he argues , the body's metabolism can no longer "cope with the speed and power, and precision of technology," but, instead, finds itself in alien environments "unplugged from its biosphere" and lost in technosocial space.[15] That is why Stelarc finds the body "obsolete," not that we could do away with it but in the sense that the notion of ego-driven body is a concept of a "simplistic, zombie-like body being driven by a psyche, mind or self" that is invalid, if it is not what Birringer calls an "expressive body" that performs and responds with the sensorial environment it is in.[16]

Stelarc, "Stimbod" performance.

So viewed, the body is not a site of inscription but a physiological structure; it is no longer an "object of desire," but, instead, an "object for redesign." Stelarc is not interested in the notion of cyborg as a body that has undergone a traumatic loss of organs and, therefore, receives implanted metallic parts, a "sci-fi, macho, military, metallic-phallic construct."[17] This projects a medical body on

[15]   Stelarc, Web interview, 1998: http://www.stelarc.va.com.au/ (19.04.2005).
[16]   Birringer, "Interacting: Performance & Transmediality," 304.
[17]   Stelarc, Web interview, 1998: http://www.stelarc.va.com.au/ (19.04.2005).

life-support systems. Instead, he sees this redesigned body as the opportunity for a multiplicity of bodies that can be separated spatially but connected electronically to become connected and thus, evolve into a greater operational entity. The internet, in Stelarc's view, is not a strategy ideal for disembodiment, since you need a physical body to be plugged into the system; instead, it offers a potential for both intimate and involuntary experiences, such as in Stelarc's use of his "Third Hand" and by his electronically wiring his own body into the internet.

By using collective infrastructures such as the internet, Stelarc achieved to be telematically—and simultaneously—present at the Pompidou Centre in Paris, the Media Lab in Helsinki and "The Doors of Perception" conference in Amsterdam. During his performance, people in these three cities could access Stelarc's body to remotely choreograph its movements via a touch-screen interface. This enabled them to enter another body, namely Stelarc's, in another place, at the same time as Stelarc's body became a "host for the behavior of remote agents."[18] Stelarc's performance could therefore be viewed as

- an early and very schematic prototype of the digital meshwork mapping anthropotechnical space as its interwoven cables, i.e. its "lines" articulating heterogeneous components produce new technosocial space in constant interaction with the map "users," the audience inducing his movements at the various touch-screen interfaces;
- proposing ways of practising agency by bringing in disturbances into a field or by generating complex emerging patterns of intertwining forces;
- strongly suggesting the necessity of theorising a new kind of spatial distribution, in which the categories "nearness" and "distance" are made "obsolete"—a word Stelarc himself likes to use when it comes to the body and bodily functions;
- an example of the interplay of socially and somatically implicated agent in an expansive and expanding spacefield which not only brings to the fore the interhuman exchange and new technological aesthetics that Birringer pointed out but also contributes to a new understanding of responsive environments;
- Stelarc's own emphasis on the importance that the body can host a "multiplicity of remote agents" would also seem to enhance not only the Communitas aspects of performance but also suggests that of the body as part of the communal.[19]

---

[18] Stelarc, performance at the Hochschule für Gestaltung und Kunst, Lucerne, 16 April 2002.
[19] Cf. Victor Turner, *The Ritual Process* (New York: Aldine de Gruyter, 1995).

Moreover, Stelarc's performance enhances the dialogic nature of agential space as the interplay between the users and the various avatars, the "outgrowths" of mathematically calculated grids of time and space, functions on the premise of socially positioned and responsive participation, namely that all parts must follow certain prescripted rules and codes.

My second example is a mapping of an immersive interactive environment called OP_ERA, developed by Rejane Cantoni and Daniela Kutschat. Adressing the problem of human-technical involvement, OP_ERA explores how and through what kind of interfaces one system may best interact with another and how we can enter and interact with a data world, from perspectives we are familiar with, without being disturbed by incalculable devices beyond our control.

OP_ERA is a world shaped as a set of interconnected logical dimensions, conceived to generate spatial cognition through multisensorial experimentation of space models evolving in relation to the human body. Its logical architecture consists of interacting dimensions structured by logical linkages. Each dimension leads to the next one and simultaneously to all previous ones. In some sense, OP_ERA has a beginning, a kind of narrative hierarchy from the first dimension to the fourth, but it has no end, nor any kind of narrative path leading from a higher dimension to a lower one. Such a structure is created with the intention to generate feedback loops, which allow events occurring in lower dimensions to affect the outcome of events in higher ones. The technological device the artists are using is the "Haptic Wall"—a SMART wall interface designed to produce tactile stimuli originating from sonic data collected by a set of microphones placed in and around the exhibit area. As soon as a microphone picks up a sound, the software samples and converts it into outputs that control sensors built into the wall.

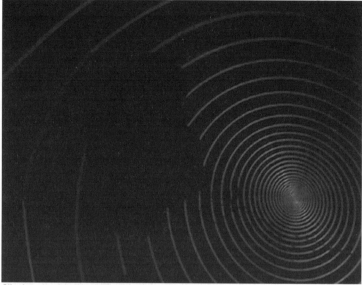

Clip 1. opera (screen shot)

The four dimensions in OP_ERA (2001 and 2003), namely X, XY, XYZ and XYZT relate to the history of spatial concepts. The first dimension, X, is a finite segment composed by a multitude of points that are sound-based elements which represent pre-programmemed computational objects that make up the world as sounds. Their nature is to transmit—attack, sustain or release from reverberation to echo—sound information. In this dimension, the user distinguishes the shape of space and his or her relative position in it by emitting and receiving sound information. Interaction or space cognition are limited to ear perception; in other words, the overall spatial concept is placed in reverberation.

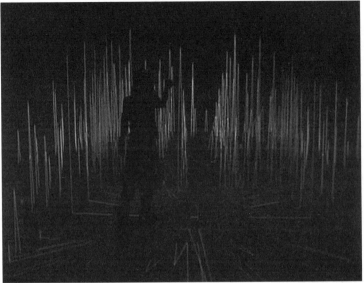

Clip 2. opera (screen shot) first dimension

The realm of the second dimension, XY, is flat. The shape of its space extends in two dimensions: the "imported" one, X, or length, plus width. Interacting by drawing the shape of space, the artists have it extend in two dimensions. All its objects "exist" only within the limits of length and width, like a huge flat screen. There are four cardinal orientation points—N, S, E, W—within this dimension. Therefore, objects and the human agent / interactor are free to move in four directions—up and down, right or left. All objects are *rendered* as light waves independently of their nature, i.e. whether they are sounds, shapes, or avatars, but *perceived* as vibrating lines, with all occupants of this dimension, including the user, having a common boundary: a space confined to a finite and limited plane. Only by touching will the human agent / interactor be able to know the actual nature of an object, whether it is a shape or a sound element. Since space in XY is confined to a finite and limited plane, the logic follows that if we try to exceed its limitations we will step out of it.

Clip 3. opera (screen shot) second dimension

The third dimension, XYZ, is a cubic realm, which turns space into an essentially empty box—a limitless void in which all things are contained and through which they move. Within this imaginary box three forms—a green triangle, a red square and a blue circle—perform a kind of Oskar Schlemmer's mathematical ballet, as the artists have suggested. All forms have various forms "behaviors" attributed to them, translating randomly according to the intrinsic qualities of their shapes. The triangle moves through the diagonals, the square through the orthogonal axes and the circle by rotating like a satellite. This ballet would go on forever were it not for the users' interaction but, as the human body is incorporated into the spatial scheme, the choreographic algorithm tracks its presence, generating responsive events by changing and flipping the plane and direction.

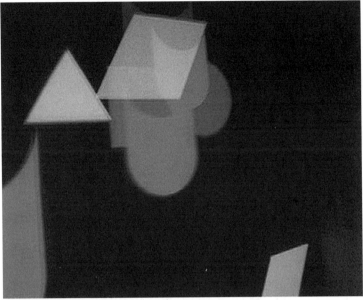

Clip 4. opera (screen shot) third dimension

In the fourth dimension, XYZ and T form a landscape evolving in time. Space is projected as a condensation of all three realms—X, XY, XYZ—composed by a multitude of emerging Lorentz attractors (three-dimensional structures corresponding to the long-term behavior of a chaotic flow) evolving in time according to the interactor's position in a complex, non-repeating pattern. In this dimension, space visualisation and cognition is only possible through simulation.

As you can see from Rejane's and Daniela's "short history of space," in this space

- the interaction human / technology is tied to the development of spatial dimensions, even limiting the potential experience of space;
- everything is spatially distributed in this responsive field, with several possible points of departure;
- the successively "folding" boundaries, though at first clearly distinguishable, suddenly either dissolve or fold into something else, interacting with the agents' positioning and perspective;
- space is set in motion by an agent introducing disturbances;
- agency is understood in terms of introducing disturbances or tracing complex patterns, with the consequence that, in such interactive motion, space in all its various forms is in constant motion—movement-space abstracted.

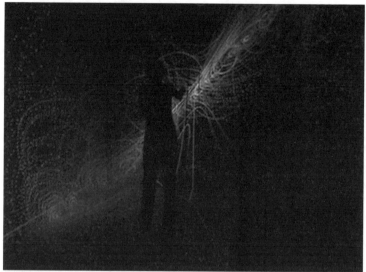

Clip 5. opera (screen shot) fourth dimension

Interactivity in these art works involves an entire environment that can only be mapped through the continuous biofeedback from the artists' sensory stimuli. What new perspectives do these new agential spaces suggest? What new positions and positionings come forth in these artist mappings? I would argue that these interactions humans—technology, the generation of what Nigel Thrift calls "qualculation"[20] demonstrate how fundamentally the new qualities based on time-space calculations are producing "new cultural conventions, techniques, forms, genres, concepts, even [...] senses." The new apprehensions of the altered time and space is what lie at the core of these artists' performances which show how agents, despite inherently implicated in social, somatic practices, are able to transfigure and transgress these by their creative imagination. We cannot get away from Cartesian space, since the mathematical calculations underlying it also provide the perspectives and projections for the responsive fields in which participating agents are at once caught up in fields transcending their immediate control and implicated in the effective exercise of their somatic, social agency. However, Cartesian space emerges *out of* these formalisations and symbolisation, rather than the other way round, that agential placements and positions emerging out of abstract Cartesian space. But what these new technologies offer are new possibilities of mapping and projecting of and by these bounded,

---

[20] Thrift, "Movement-Space," 593.

situated agents who are not so bounded and circumscribed that they are not able to transfigure this space by their creative imagination.

As mentioned earlier, all map reading is indexical from the aspect that it refers a) to the relationship between user and map invalid and b) to the relationship between the map and its referents. In cyberspace, there is yet another indexical aspect. Because, although these various attempts to map technosocial space in digital art involve highly sophisticated technologies, the participants nevertheless need a physical body for the interactive experience, which means that they need to be indexically, i.e. referentially anchored. Interacting in virtual space, the participant becomes a biocybernetic body, divided into two complementary media: one body which remains carnal and "real" in the environment it exists, and its avatar, which is the virtual, disembodied projection of the "real" body.[21] Although we might seem to momentarily lose ourselves in cyberspace, our physical body remains carnal and "real." That is what makes it possible for us to maintain proprioception, the sensation of self from within the body.

Although the medium of digital art is fundamentally self-referential, as are our digital maps and may seem virtually non-indexical, there must still be reference in order for us not to lose ourselves in cyber- and antropo-technical space. However, in this agential space with its ceaseless intermeshing of various agents, life becomes a meshwork of successive foldings. It is not a network of connectors, since this environment cannot be bounded but is a constantly expanding space along which we live our lives as a transformative process. That is why mapping this new space requires different strategies because what we are mapping is a world of processes, of continuous numerical calculations and of nomadologic movement of transformation and change.

---

[21] Cf. Lucia Santaella, *Culturas e artes do pós-humano: Da cultura das mídias à cibercultura* (São Paulo: Paulus, 2003).

Benjamin H. Bratton

The Aesthetics of Logistics: Architecture, Subjectivity & the Ambient Database

1. Soft Space: Introduction

Picture a computer sitting on a desk, its glowing monitor staring at you. Some designers, we call them programmemers and interaction designers, are experts at designing what happens inside the glowing glass rectangle, the software that turns this one glass surface into an interface to global information networks. Other designers, we call them architects, are experts at designing what happens outside the glowing glass rectangle, the physical structures that provide structure to the regularities of habitation. However, we don't actually experience this inside and outside differentiation as strictly as this division of labour would have it. We live with one in relation to the other. Some designers and strategists, not so many as of yet, work to define what happens inside the monitor as a function of what happens outside of it, (software as a function of the architecture), and what happens outside as a function of the inside (architecture as a function of the software). This line of thinking and working requires seeing architecture not as a static form, but as a kind material procedure in the staging of extremely dynamic networks, and it also forces us to work with software as something (always already) physical, spatial and embodied (as opposed to mental, placeless and virtual).

Software exists in the world with us, determining and deriving operations of place and mobility. Your car starts because of the software in it, the gas pump delivers because of the software in it, the traffic lights police driving because of the software that runs

   The print version of this essay is accompanied by an online version which includes links to illustrations indicated within the text and other additional material. The online version is at http://www.cultureindustry.com/bratton/logistics

them, and you arrive on time because of the software in your watch, phone or handheld computer, etc. Software, as surely as glass or steel, is a building block of modern space. It is both a mode and a means of production (and consumption) in the network society. In this, the capacity to communicate through the media of software has produced a kind of "class" dynamic, in which one's relationship to the productive and consumptive operations of software (to speak through it and be spoken through it) to some extent determine the positions through which one may live in the world with these social infrastructures. The "database" is a peculiar form of this. It resides almost always out of sight, one rarely if ever actually sees how one's identity is processed by its operations, and yet the results of its organising calculations can be read in the very arrangement of the world we live in. Databases determine what goes where, and when it gets there, how it gets there and sometimes why it gets there. They operate, like a silent animating agency, just beneath the surface of the prosaic contemporary object (and increasingly body).

The logics of this animation are surely patterned, and are legible to us as figural systems to such a degree that it is impossible *not* to understand its agency as (among other things) an *aesthetic* technology. The database arranges the world—providing access, sequentiality, repetition, variability, individuation, classification, bordering—according not just to instrumentality and calculation, but more importantly according to multiple modes of cultural and discursive legibility. As such a "database aesthetics" should not limit its inquiry just to the consideration of the database itself as aesthetic form (its discourse of attribute, value, table, etc.) nor as an agent in the production of other "aesthetic" digital media (such as database film, literature or art) but must attend with utmost care to how the database operates, figuratively and physically, in the material production of cultural habitat and the resolutions of durable architectures of form and object that characterise it.

Such a position only complicates how we would understand the multiple and incongruous ways in which software and architecture encounter one another, and more importantly how people and societies engage themselves in the midst of these encounters. There are, in these collisions and becomings, all sorts of translation problems. What something means in one place or inside one screen (on the surface of a building perhaps) is not the same everywhere and changes how something else can signify (a menu option in a GUI), and certainly is as open to as much subjective improvisation as any confluence of language and technology. The translations, through subjects and by subjects, of software into architecture and back again, are then the matter under consideration here. Conceptualisation of these translations has resulted in several sociocultural theories of computation, some of much greater lasting value than others. The least useful, though perhaps among the most visible of these, render computation as a *virtual* (immaterial, insubstantial, decorporeal) formation, as opposed to a virtual-becoming (immanent, emergent, physical). These "Cartesian" models of "social software" (from usability theory, to new media as new cinema, to gaming/VR, etc.) do have important things to tell us about what new things there are to see, but are fatally limited by the preoccupation that what is crucial about software is primarily an issue for *visual* culture, and that theories of subject to be derived are about "seeing subjects." What is most important about these translations may be invisible, if also obviously more physical (more on this below). Equally problematic, within a conventional Media Arts context, is the preoccupation with moments of mutual formation between subjects and software focused on the moments and manners in which subjects are in the mode of being "on line," (browser users, email users, game users, etc.) as opposed to doing other things equally dependent on software (like driving a car, cashing a paycheque, buying a banana or crossing a border).

Without suspending the obvious power of spectral and the imaginary, it is clear that the physicality of computation as an element of the everyday world is less representational than presentational, less cinematic than environmental, less cognitive than dialogic. Such a position is in conversation with Slajov Žižek's interest in "how computerisation effects the hermeneutic horizon of our everyday experience."[1] Žižek argues against the "postmodern" ideology of cyberspace as a kind of wholly transparent, decorporealised "frictionless field," and on behalf of the Lacanian (and laconic) Real where subjects and their symptoms, however decentred, are only more complicated and complicit in their own interface-driven status as the partial-objects of the Other. It is in precisely "these threatened limit-surfaces" that we are interested here, but instead of leaving, as Žižek does (in this particular essay), the matter with a conclusion that software makes the Other both further away and more proximate, the technical conditions of the world both more opaque and more transparent, and ultimately complicates beyond certain recognition the natural and the artificial, we instead begin the question not from the subject and its "object relations," but instead with the partial object and its "subject relations." All the more complicated, you will see, when the

---

[1] Slavoj Žižek, "Cyberspace, or the Unbearable Closure of Being," *The Plague of Fantasies* (London: Verso Press, 1997) 133.

partial objects in question (architecture, software, in particular) are enrolled as both actors and actants (see Latour)[2] in the dramas of the subject.

Of these, the database (the topic of this volume) is a unique "linguistic" form, and a unique form of physical software. Databases produce space in their image (and the possible examples are numerous and familiar). Go into a supermarket and roster the shelves and their contents. You are walking around inside a database. Everything you see and where you see it, and how you see it is a function of this physical-discusive calculation. Indeed the very aesthetic of display is too reminiscent (too object-orientated even) not to imagine the place itself as a physical spreadsheet, a concrete rectangular DBMS in which you can stand and ambulate. It would be inappropriate to understand the impact(s) of the database on aesthetics (and vice versa) by looking only at "cultural" media like cinema, art and literature. In fact, the database can and sometimes does configure the entire human habitat in its image, automatic but strategic, general but individuated, networked but located. Though my examples will focus primarily in the conversions of software and subjectivity in relation to *architecture*, database aesthetics is as crucial to the discourses of organisational studies, political science, mechanical engineering or any other discipline of social design as it is to the pursuit of other more traditionally cultural innovations.

Several interpretive positions inspire the configurations of software, space and subjectivity presented below, and while I cannot fully elucidate each here, it of use to be clear about the larger theoretical trajectories this essay imagines itself in dialogue (if not always agreement). For some readers, such acknowledgements will serve as subtextual shorthand for arguments made between the lines, and for others perhaps an impetus to read (or reread them in a new context). After Ulrich Beck and Scott Lash's *reflexive modernisation*, the massive transcoding of institutional and organisational forms into the images and bodies of software is a fundamental means and end of a "second modernisation" whereby the structures and operations of Modernity are themselves undergoing a general (though highly heterogeneous and irregular) process of re-modernisation.[3] This transcoding and translation can be seen as a means by which Žižek's "computerisation" both disembeds and reembeds the constitutions of the Modern. Bruno Latour,

---

[2] Cf Bruno Latour, *Reassembling the Social: An Introduction to Actor-Network-Theory* (Oxford: Oxford University Press, 2005).

[3] Scott Lash, Ulrich Beck and Anthony Giddens, *Reflexive Modernization* (Cambridge: Polity Press, 1994).

John Law and Michel Callon's *actor-network theory* allows the implicitly Deleuzean circuits of subjective and objective configuration a more social and empirical frame.[4] For this, the agency of the subject and the subject of agency are located as much in the surfaces, artefacts and contingent affordances of the material world as in the symptomatic tendencies of phenomenal subjects. Habitats are the site and the result of polyphonous quasi-objects, quasi-subjects and variously static and dynamic mesh-network conditions. Latour's network and the spaces (and times) of flow for which it allows is considerably less Humanistic and economistic than Manuel Castells's connotation, the certain importance of which the reader is probably more familiar.[5] Thirdly, the reflexivity of the reflectability between software, subject and space is understood according technologies of *mimesis*, both linguistic and corporeal. Philippe Lacoue-Labarthe locates the possibility of the subject in the mediations of its echoes, and the literatures of its self-description, while Judith Butler physicalises these doublings in the repetition of bodily performances (both mechanical and theatrical) as the system through which the experience of significance (and vice versa) literally takes place.[6] This is related to but far from identical to the logics of *habitus* as elucidated by Pierre Bourdieu, for whom the repetition of bodily-identification (let us say 'habit) and the semi-durability of social material space ('habitat') cooperate in both producing and consuming the multiple little violences of practice.

The specificity of software within these frameworks is complex. Despite (and perhaps because of the dot com crash) the social, economic and cultural importance of "software" is only becoming greater. This momentum is fed both by global economic growth and recession, and by both cosmopolitan and fundamentalist cultural markets, and is remaking language, the object (and the language-object, and the object of language) in its image, and does so mainly invisibly, as infrastructure, as *precondition* of action.

---

[4] Latour explicitly indicates the debt of Actor-Network Theory to the work of Deleuze in an interview with Hugh Crawford, *Configurations* 1.2 (1993): 247-268. "Actor-network theory should be called actant/rhizome ontology," he says.

[5] See, for example, Manuel Castells, "The Rise of the Network Society," *The Information Age: Economy, Society and Culture,* vol. I. (Oxford: Blackwell, 1996)

[6] See Latour, *We Have Never Been Modern* (Cambridge, Mass.: Harvard University Press, 1993); John Law and John Hassard, eds. *Actor Network Theory and After* (London: Blackwell, 1999); Lacoue-Labarthe, *Typography: Mimesis, Philosophy, Politics* (Stanford: Stanford University Press, 1989); Judith Butler, *Bodies That Matter: On the Discursive Limits of "Sex"* (London: Routledge, 1993); Pierre Bourdieu, *Outline of a Theory of Practice* (Cambridge: Cambridge University Press, 1977). Butler differentiates her own theory of repetition form Bourdieu's in "Performativity's Social Magic" in *Bourdieu: A Critical Reader,* ed. Richard Shusterman (London: Blackwell, 1999) 113-128.

While the scope of this essay casts its interest widely across the integrating material cultures of software, the mediate productions of individual and collective identification and technological transformations in the professional discipline of architecture, its purpose for a particular reader is actually rather quite specific and pragmatic. Design, one hopes, is a practice of practicality, of translating insight into instrument. Conceptual formation precedes material design, feeding into it, and material design informs conceptual reformation: the cycles of practical theory name both the practices and the results of "design."

2. City: Habitat, Database, Subject

I begin at the beginning. Software is simultaneously a language, a technology and a system of collective representation. Like every modern institution over the last couple of decades, urban/architectonic forms have undergone a transformation *in the image of software*. Increasingly, cityforms are modelled not just *with* software but also *out of* software. Architectural design operates according to the manipulation of digital forms. Architecture, as infrastructure, is reconfigured as a distributed field of interfaces and databases; some visible and some invisible, some handheld, some embedded in environmental material, some deep into the urban core. The urban distribution of databases dislodges and reframes (respatialises and retechnologises) social action and the design agendas that are elaborated from it. This condition refocuses design problematics on the *reflexive* interplays between cultural forms, architectural forms and technological affordances (between subjectivity, space and software), and locates the complexities of each in and always *conditional* relation to the others. Each figure (subjectivity, space and software) produces the design horizons of the others, the form and limit of each as both habit and habitat. The linguistic, technological and corporeal terms of each *transpose* and *transcode* the operations of the others to affect a preliminary index of mutually constitutive conditions. This material reflexivity between subjectivity, space and software, as a *database envelope* through which conditional modes of subjectivity are manifested, presents itself in a threefold arrangement:

Space (Subjectivity, Software)
Urban-architectonic space is modelled not only as infrastructure for media, or as a metaphor for mediation, but as a generative condition of both the subjective bodies that mobilise and inhabit it, and for the visible and invisible software forms that envelope them.

Subjectivity (Software, Space)

The mobile subject of urban space both models/is modelled by the transcoding of bodily habits into interfaces and by the generative grammars of databases as figurative discourses and (invisible) urban infrastructure.

Software (Subjectivity, Space)

Embedded/mobile interfaces and ambient databases both represent the social and objective forms they mediate, and in turn generate the material discursive figures of those forms. Subjectivities are modelled as databases, and inhabit urban spaces, which are generated/deployed as database operations, which are themselves based on the transcoding of subjective thought and habit.

3. Transcoding

First, a practical definition is appropriate. In that software is both a form of language and a form of technology, it must be understood according to both genealogies. One writes software, interacts with it linguistically, but in doing so is able to deploy these linguistic forms as technologies of action, production and construction. Friedrich Kittler famously prescribes that in today's society, citizens must be able to speak, write and communicate in at least two languages, one natural and one artificial. The artificial languages of C++, Java, and various scripting languages such as Perl, constitute a linguistic infrastructure for a globalised culture of production generative of every institution reliant on software for the internal and external communication of its data and its processes, which is to say nearly every institution. Programmemers who are unable to interact in natural languages such as English or Russian can nevertheless communicate and collaborate on highly complex projects built in a commonly understood programmeming language. Software, as a language, is able to bridge entrenched cultural differences.

But the technologisation of language is equally crucial as the "linguification of technology" for the use and consumption of software and its production. Conventional human activities and institutions are translated into software. Recent years can be characterised as a time in which nearly all institutions (from running a company, to guarding a border, to planning a building, to managing one's personal time) have been translated, *transcoded*, into the terms and operations of software. "Transcoding" is the name Lev Manovich gives to the discursive transposition of cultural operations into computational operations, and vice versa. The transcoding of forms between the "computer layer" to the "human layer" is, according to Manovich, the circuit by which technological form moves to take on the qualities of human forms, and cultural forms operate computational processes.[7] For example, the graphical user interface employs and elaborates several cultural metaphors (desktop, trash can, saving into folders, etc.) enabling people (now "users") to execute and manipulate complex computational operations according to a virtualisation of already understood cognitive habits.

Manovich's connotation of *transcoding* operates between what he calls the "cultural and computer layers" within a particular piece of software. I employ the notion to describe soft space *transcoding* operates between cultural, institutional forms in the "real world" and their transpositions into the linguistic technologies of software. That is, the linguistic transposition is not only between interface and application layers (between interface and machine languages within a given piece of software) but also between the subjective bodily spaces and their computational analogues. The reflexive counter-production is between architecturally sited cultures and the softwares they animate and which animate them. The reflection works both ways. For example, in order for systematic complexities of managing an enterprise to be conducted through software, they must first be codified and translated, *transcoded*, into the terms and operators of software: revenue becomes an input variable, payroll an output variable, etc. The entire socio-economic structure of the enterprise is simulated, digitised, and translated into a condition of networked data and interfaces. This process in turn comes to *redetermine* the actual cultural and economic operations of the enterprise, reversing the direction of reflection. Software virtualises the organisation and then the organisation comes to mimic the structures, discourses and demands of the software.

Below, I consider the production of soft space and its realisation in the reflexive transcodings of architectural forms (from surface to city), computational forms (interface to database), and subjective forms (collective to self to body). This tripling of interrelations of coding multiplies the complexity of reflexive processes at work in the spatial manifestation of the database as a social form. We will site this tripled reflexivity according to (1) mutually-embedded, conditional productions of embodied subjectivity as both a determination and an effect of material architectonic context and the discursive, environmental materiality of the database, (2) of architectural programme and topography as determination and effect of embodied subjectivity and spatially contextualised data

---

[7] Lev Manovich, *The Language of New Media* (Cambridge, Mass.: MIT Press, 2001).

forms, and (3) of databases as a determination and effect of the subjectivities they index and the built spaces constructed in their image and interest.

4. Database: Reflexivity[8]

The apocalyptic hoopla surrounding the "Y2K bug" was a turning point in the general appreciation of computation's spatial ubiquity. This "global typo" in which countless infrastructural technologies were delimited by an arbitrary digitalisation of the centurial cycle, was not only a practical grammatical failure but also one which promised that the inaccurate sum of the invisible computational processes surrounding us would directly manifest itself as a comprehensive failure in the systemic regularity of the entire social world. After this quasi-imaginary prophecy had come and passed, the *spatial personality* of computation was mainstreamed. Computation was no longer something that only sits on desks, it was broadly recognised as a intangible fabric of the environment, a building block of habitat, an elemental force of things and their movements.[9] The Y2K bug was a "linguistic" slip that had "technological" consequences; and it is this convertibility between linguistic representation and technological form that makes software (perhaps) unique as both a semiotic system of production and as a feature-operation of the built environment. To be sure, this mimetic reflexivity between quasi-autonomous signification on the

---

[8] The discursive form of the database might be traced back at least as far as Leibniz' description of the "compossible matrix," but the career of the database as a physical environmental materiality had to wait until the proliferation of digital computation as a general technology of information to be realised.

[9] The location of the database in trajectories of philosophical inquiry discloses much about the nature of the inquiry and the social condition of its proposition. In the canonical *The Postmodern Condition: A Report on Knowledge*, (Minneapolis: University of Minnesota Press, 1985) Jean-François Lyotard links a general social momentum toward a digitalisation of forms, the displacement of the authoritative depth of the archive by the reflexive totality of the database, with the historical dissolution of master, grand narratives and the extant proliferation of local, micronarrative knowledge forms. In *The Mode of Information: Poststructuralism and Social Context* (Chicago: University of Chicago Press, 1990) the first comprehensive portrait of post-68 social philosophy in the reflected image of post-68 media technologies, Mark Poster employs Michel Foucault's notion of a generalised panopticon to cast the database not as post-political apparatus of heterological decentralisation, but rather as an imprisoning digital envelope of surveillance. Through Poster's reading, the very mode of production in a digital society is the differential control of information as a means of surveillance and the enforcement of conformity. For example, Lyotard, writing in 1984, looks at the opposition of capitalism and communism as an end game between two terminal metanarratives, whereas Poster's point of reference, writing after the fall of the Wall and the subsequent immolations of Stalinism is the East German Stasi, and a self-surveilling society in the image of a carnivorous database.

one hand and physical form on the other is not an abstraction, but rather an active process which both locates and is located in the structured improvisations of everyday life.[10]The threat of catastrophic removal makes more visible what it endangers.

Software is always somewhere, is always encountered in place; and place is always already conditioned by software. The proliferation of software and of interfaces as materials of habitat, as sure and strong as glass and steel, continues even as "architecture" remains loyal to the (even digital) conception of blank structures and abstract forms into which and upon which information technologies might be latter retrofitted by specialised technicians. And so the encounter between software programme and architectural programme largely remains merely a tactical if not wholly improvised juxtaposition, a situational suturing accomplished by user/inhabitants in the field, on the fly and often against the grain of the software, the hardware and the architectural design-condition. Nevertheless, the largely *ad hoc* hybridisations emerging from this prosaic bricolage of digital and material space do generate sorts of "informal forms" that demonstrate the pliabilities of computational space to the idiosyncratic needs and desires of embodied user-inhabitants. What becomes clear from these encounters of necessity is that the architectural condition of the ambient database is organised not only by a rote iteration of inflexible tools, but also by performative encounters between local problematics of subjectivity, software and space. This definition and production of computation as an environmental configuration, a habitat, supposes the parallel definition and production of inhabitants appropriately tuned to the specific demands of this mode of inhabitation. Just as the empty sculptural forms of architecture only come to life as they are lived in, as they particularly and idiosyncratically stage subjective embodiments of place, the activation of any user-facing, user-directed software requires a user to activate it, to understand it, to think though and work with it. As such these tactical employments of pervasive computation are predicated upon the conditional, systemic production of subject positions that blend or juxtapose 'user' and 'inhabitant.' In this, the embodied stages of architecture become a computational field, encoding their own *doxic* logics, and refigure the mobile habitation of place as a 'user' position. Likewise, these dispositions of differen-

---

[10] This is understood in relation to Maurice Merleau-Ponty's notion of the bridge between bodily space and the spatialised body. See his *Phenomenology and Perception* (London: Routledge, 1962).

tial interaction become habitat, solidifying their location as a situated, enveloping form.[11]

Clearly the production of subjectivities in relation to these solutions remains as ever a *reflexive* operation. As the dispositional mobility of the inhabitant is framed and tethered by the condensation of intentions slated within the specifically embedded interface, the structural (and infrastructural) "hailing" of the user/subject is opened and limited by the differential temporalities of architectonic embodiment. But precisely how this interplay unfolds cannot be causally located in only the semiotic discursivity of software, in the landscape of built space, or in the temporal intentionality of embodiment, but rather in the dynamic, mimetic co-systematicity of all three. As the Y2K bug episode makes plain, the necessity of the circuit between these two is perhaps most *dramatic* when their coordination is absent: (1) when the environmental embeddedness of the software is disconnected from its encounter with intentional actors, (2) when the environmental embeddedness of the software is disconnected from the specific architectural conditions of place, or (3) when the architectural stage for information technology is disconnected from the user/inhabitant's needs and intentions. That is to say, we see it best when it not working.

What such disconnections foreground to us are the necessary contextual interrelations between each term of this reflexive mimesis—*subjectivity, space and software*.[12] The three sections below specifically define each operation, and structure this reflexive interrelation as an irreducible condition of their mutual production and organisation.

5. Subjectivity: Space, Software
Subjectivity into Space. Social subjects, cultural subjects, are always already subject *positions*, existing and operating in relative distanced relation to other subjects and other object relations. To speak and to act as a subject is to do so through (or even against) a particular position and field of positions. The production of subjectivity *takes place* within an active, ongoing, differential complex of technologies and media. Different media technologies allow for different subject figures, and as such contribute to the specific definition of different cultures of interaction, expression and con-

[11] This should not be understood only as a (Heideggerian) instrumentalism, but as a event-moment that makes new subjects through new tools and new kinds of embodiment, the horizons of which are expressive.

[12] See my "Accounting and Pervasive Computation," *Afterimage, The Journal of Media Arts and Cultural Criticism* 30.1 (2006): 13-14.

sumption. Subjects speak through the specific channels of the technologies at hand, and are, at the same moment, spoken through them. Likewise, subjects are always already embodied subjects, living in and as particular enunciations of an embodied condition. Embodied subjects live in the world *habitually*, performing a routine of postures and circuits through space that wear grooves into the material world, producing artefacts of a subject's presence and leaving traces in and as a habitat. Design is historically predicated and principled on matching artificial forms to bodily need and sensory pleasure. In this, design is politicised by the fact that those forms don't just mimic bodies but train them as well. Environments configure and constrain the ongoing formation of subjects by differentially positioning bodies and the conditions of their performances. Habits produce habitats, habitats produce habits; subjectivity is both a condition and an outcome of this cycle, as sensual as it is functional.

Consider that as archaeologists decipher architectural debris, and in doing so are able to characterise social cultures that produce and were produced by these artefacts, architecture must be understood as the durable residue of particular modes of collective habitation played out at an upon its material forms and deformations. But particular configurations of spatial form are of course not just random artefactual residue (polymorphic debris cast in place by the summation of all things that happened there) they are concretisations of the deliberate creative design of *architects*. As such, habitats are the elaborations of particular conventions of design and *programme*. Programme, the predictive organisation and division of architectonic space into different modes of use and encounter (display, storage, gathering, circulation, bodily function, etc.) contains within it, necessarily and inevitably, a direct and specific argument about how a particular structure will stage the activities of collective habit and habitation (performance, not just behaviour). Programme proposes an argument about the quality of individual and collective embodiment and how they operate within a functionally differentiated field of architectural space.

This metacode of architectural programme and the overdetermination of subjectivity it presumes is an operative fiction employed always only incompletely by those who work through it. Programme is never completely activated according to plan, never resolved, but rather, like every determining structure, is always evaded, customised and modulated by the prosaic requirements and experiments of actual use in context. Programme stages an encounter between subject positions it can only very conditionally contain. Of equal importance to the metacode of programme as

important is the tactical activation of programmemed and unpro-
grammemed space *against* itself by those who inhabit it; action is
staged by programme but limited by it only in the exceeding of the
behavioural thresholds it provides, the definition of a deviation from
it. Space, as collective dwelling, is customised, reconfigured, con-
tested, and fought over. It is as overwritten by *improvisation of
inhabitation* as it is by intentional or enforceable design.

These uses and counter-uses, designs and embodiments, solutions and dissolutions, can be read as the sited collision of
inevitably incongruous subject positions, differentially empowered
to repeat, enforce and institutionalise their claims over a given site.
Architecture is (perhaps foremost) a technology of collective representation and of the visible and invisible contestations this entails.
It mediates collective abstract bodies as much as individual anato-
mies: the legal subjectivities of the State or an administration, the
experiential expressions of a corporation's brand identity, the design personality of an architect, the material figure of its function,
etc. But while these official physical discourses of space both drive
and derive architecture from their authorities and stage the conditional positions within it, the environment 'as lived' is configured
and modulated in the private manoeuvres of those who course its
interiors, touch its surfaces and dwell there.

Subjectivity into Software. Like architecture (and sometimes instead of architecture) software mediates several incongruous
modes of embodied and cognitive subjectivity, among them, in its
current institutional cultural form, a condensation of the *microeconomic subject*, "he who *is* his calculation of buying and selling."
The acquisition and application of software-related skills is a crucial
strategy of selfhood in the network society. Software acumen,
broadly considered and specifically employed, defines not only the
practical means with which to work and communicate in a soft-
ware-based economy, it also technologises the very social location
of that work into its terms and fields. Because of its importance in
both the definition and acquisition of economic capital in the network economy software also serves to redefine the quality and
character of social and symbolic capital in its own image. Software
positions social subjects within particular relations as *users*, providing both a medium for their interaction and a grammar for the very
construction of their symbolic interactions within the field of contemporary ("office") space. Software functions as both a medium
of habit and a material of habitat, and drives this progression of
subject formation from both directions. It is employed as a language of action and expression, and as a medium of

communication, through which everyday life is performed. As an animate environmental force, as linguistic interface and as logistical technology—on screens and off screens, visibly and invisibly—software both concretises and limits the production of subjectivity in its own image.

The interface, understood as a skin of disembodied intentions, visualises the array of sequential postures and activities as a reduced frame of virtual miniatures. The complexity of embodied performativity is narrowed and functionally instrumentalised into repeatable cycles of information manipulation, ones legible and comprehendible to the user/inhabitant because they repeat, virtually, a compressed choreography of that activity's analogue as physical *habit*. This is not to say that the interface necessarily overdetermines life undertaken through it. Even as a disembodied skin of dispositions, and to some extent precisely because of its instrumentality, the interface operates and is operated upon by the user like any other technology; that is, tactically, improvisationally, specifically.[13] Because it is a mass medium, the graphical user interface radically generalises its virtualisation of a given activity and the subject position constructed through it. The "I" construed through the general interface is a generic subjectivity. But both as a technology and as a linguistic form, the interface is worked upon and sometimes worked against by the user to idiosyncratic ends. One's unique personal knowledge about how a process works in the "real" world, when done "by hand" recommends itself as a specific "virtual" solution, sometimes completely across the grain of the preconceived "use-cases" from which interfaces are architected and synthesised. Because it is generic, the virtual habit organised in the GUI is only a *programme* of actions and interactions, one as available to counter-habitation as any other form of architecture.

---

[13] The METRO Group Future Store Initiative is a cooperation project between METRO Group, SAP and Intel as well as other partner companies from the information technology and consumer goods industries. See http://www.future-store.org

Figure 1: (a) The habitual activities of economic interaction are materialised into built space, cast as an environmental institution. That institutionalisation of action in the bodies and discourses of the microeconomic subject parallels the proliferation of generic spatial accommodations (action into architecture into software ... into action); (b) Sony MagicLink Interface. The desktop metaphor is elaborated from the two-dimensional version of Windows to one in which the virtual body is actually bent and sitting in front of an array of recognisable icon-objects. Peculiar that a handheld device that allows he user to be mobile positions the user discursively as virtually desk-bound and inert.

This production is a "transcoding" of the subjective forms and habits of specific fields into the discursive structures of software. Elsewhere I have examined this in light of Pierre Bourdieu's theory of *habitus* and considered how the design and deployment of software interaction systems involves a miniaturisation and technologisation of *habitus*.[14] But in that the interface condenses both an array of habitual actions and also stages them according to their embedding in particular fields, there are in fact two such miniaturisations at work. The first transcoding is "cognitive" and the second is "architectonic." The "cognitive" transcoding allows for the intentional execution of complex computational processes through the manipulation of visual interface elements that visualise and virtualise such operations. For example, because the user understands how to throw things away, how the particular exercise of subtracting elements from being immediately at hand is to place them in a discrete, concave void, "trashcan" icons allow for the erasing of files from a hard drive. Without overlaying one cognitive habit into and onto the interface, the near universal legibility of file erasure from data storage drives would be less possible. But the reverse may be as true: cross-cultural and cross-generational variation does direct us toward moments in which physical trashcans are legible because trashcan icons are already used and understood! As described above, either condition of practical legibility is one of performative *repetition*, of habitual postures and regular ac-

---

[14] Pierre Bourdieu, *Outline of a Theory of Practice* (Cambridge: Cambridge University Press, 1977). See http://www.spacesyntax.com

tivities. As said, embodied subjects make circuits with the world, employing parts of it in idiosyncratic ways. The interface layer (of Office-ware to continue the example) between the user/inhabitant and the software operations is a portrait of a particular *doxic* script of the habitual activities appropriate to the mediate and immediate actions at hand (in/as the user/inhabitant of office actions).

The architectural transcoding, (which I consider more completely in the section, *software into space*) miniaturises and virtualises the spatial conditions of the field and the correlative activities that take place there. The desktop, for example, is not only a cognitive field it is a particular social organisation of *dividuated* bodies and generic responsibility. The 'office' field that provides an implicitly or explicitly surrounding metacontext for the desktop condenses a particular regime of scripts for individual and collective activity there. In offices, one is there to work, not play. Accordingly, Office-ware arbitrates the computational capacity of applications and hardware into a discursive technology appropriate not only to the habits of work but also to the subjective location of its performance: office *spaces*. Officeware is an interface not only to particular activities virtualised and employed by computation, but also to particular spaces in which those activities are collaboratively staged and managed. (See figure 1)

6. Space: Subjectivity, Software

Space into Subjectivity. Architecture may be defined (or refined) as the materialisation of spatial abstraction into the built environment of social life. The architect, or rather architecture as a "mode of practice," casts spaces into real place, and in doing so reforms the actual structural character of the social, reforms its builtness at the material level of solidity and form. Architecture, as programme and as technology of collective representation, *derives* bodies, individual and collective, through its formations. Programme concretised in built form stages the conditions through which and around which the possibilities of subjectivity can ever unfold. Architecture, literally in the surfaces and corridors of its form, engineers and dramatises the positions and dispositions of communication that might emerge in and as its interior effects. In this, architecture does not merely represent psychic machinations, stand for them metaphorically, it *presents* them, materialises them. Subjects are always already subject positions; and architecture, as the durable field of positions, is, in the syntactical contours of its sensate enveloping, the condition through which embodiment events itself in the world. Inverting the deconstructivist moment, language is a metaphor for architecture.

Architecture's corpographies and choreographies of location stage both very general and very specific embodied subjects, and in doing so fashion public and private programmes for both the collective body in general ("corporation") and in specific ("IBM") and the individual body in general ("hotel room") and in specific ("home"). The modulation between generalisation and specificity is the *content* of spatial context and contextualisation, itself conducted by the performative framings of architectural programme. This "enworlding" of experience takes place as a highly contingent and volatile reflexive circuit. But as ever, the communication is refusable. As I have suggested already, to re-perform, consciously or unconsciously, a role within those afforded by a site is to accept a sort of requisite structural inscription as the (provisionally) legitimate position for one's body(ies) within those geographies and borderings. To employ a dusty phrase, architecture inevitably *hails subjects*, and does so through all the multiple grammars of internal and external globalisation." This is why acting against the assignment of role makes itself known as an action against specific spatialisations.

Just as the repetition of habit produces, as extant inscription, a "groove" in the figural contours of the built environment, and in fact builds the environment precisely through such repetitions, habitats in turn produce and enunciate themselves though bodies, manifested as habits. Spaces contain and constrain. Spaces are not just expressions of bodily form; they also express themselves as and through bodily form (prisoner, worker, individual, mass). Habitats (cage, desk, car, savannah, bed, corridor, etc.) condition and are the condition of the production of bodily habits, and of the collective representation of those habits institutionalising themselves as material culture. As Foucault (for one) made plain in the 1960's, power describes and inscribes itself architectonically. The political programme of the Modernist impulse in architecture was/is to fashion a better world by fashioning better modes of habitation. In the design and enforcement of preferred modes of dispositional embodiment, by fashioning better habitat forms, the political body can be trained to operate, to fill itself out, in a particular way. For example, States describe the form and limit of citizen subjects in how they physically and discursively address the inhabitants of courts, capital buildings, voting booths and jail cells.

Space into software. Traditionally, architecture is the conception of inhabitable but empty sculptures on cleared, singular sites. In these sculptures, inhabitants may encounter several sorts of screens, and on them information content of various origin and meaning. The *dwelling* functions of these screen events, however, are usually not considered as primary to the architectonic programme at hand. According to this, media are placed in, or perhaps merely *on* architecture. Similarly, media design is conventionally limited to the definition and deployment of the content that exists within the frame of those various screens, regardless of specific location. Media architecture might then be simply understood as the integration of these two incomplete design mandates, of programmeming inside and outside the frame of the screen. This working definition of media architecture would include the design of differentially (dis)integrated site-screen events: electronic, physical, embedded, local, and transmitted duration-structures. Across these, the design palette of media architecture is, it would be said, the *displacement of time and the delay of space.*

Building systems are located scenarios for the experience of both mediate and physical habitats, some "here and now," some "there and then": the ambient environment is built (infra)structure for media and information experience design. Across both deliberate and accidental networks, media architectonics configures/coordinates modulating informational compressions and expansions of spatial and temporal organisation. Traditionally architecture is designed to accommodate particular social and logistic operations, but its conception as a context for interfaces, themselves elaborations of the deeper contexts of local and networked spatial cultures, remains a more provisional endeavour. Just as this decentralisation might also be a despecifying of architectonic location and its specific programme from the interface condition of the generalised terminal (the screen that can screen any and all interfaces), it is also an augmentation of particular sites and the range of activities that they can and do stage (the living room is a bank, my phone is a bank, etc.) and in doing so evolve with the landscape as a socio-linguistic horizon.

Figure 2: (a) Bloomberg space-time. The space of the screen is rendered both geo-graphically (as a landscape of image, text, data in narrative juxtaposition), and temporally (as a continuous multiple of evolving flows). For print media, advertising interrupts space and for televisual media, advertising interrupts sequence. In Bloomberg Space-time both are interpenetrated into a kind of radically self-simultaneous "content"; (b) Bloomberg Surface 1: The Lobby from Thomas Leeser's proposal for the Eybeam Atelier Museum in Chelsea, Manhattan. The self-simultaneous flows of the Bloomberg screen are deployed as (and on) architectural programme. The spatial inhabitant is modelled as a "viewser" (broadband speak for user + viewer) and their intentionalities for space are rendered as traceable use-cases; (c) Bloomberg Surface 2: design office + imaginary forces, IBM interactive multimedia conference table. The Office *hexis* is virtualised into Office-ware and here dissimulated (resimulated?) and screened back onto the surfaces of the office habitat, here encountered quite literally as itself a screen.

In this, it is not just that the embedded interface is a reduced, en-coded version of the architectural programme in play, rather the very site itself is understood as the manifestation of both present and virtual flows of software, all of which produce the conditions of location within the contexts of global emplacement and dis-placement. Location-specific computation, and the embedded interface systems that mediate them to user/inhabitants, translate these choreographic modulations into a lexicon of word/actions available to the user/inhabitant to activate the encoded program-mematic potentialities of a given surface/envelope. The latent, generative code of a site's architectonic programme is made mani-fest in the linguistic expressions of the condensed interfaces that transpose the surfaces of objects and buildings into lan-guage/technologies. For example, a bank, as pillars, concrete, teller windows, etc. an architectural institutionalisation of the abstract machine of *banking*, defined as the centralisation and maintenance and dispersal of investment capital made more or less liquid. The ATM machine, situated on the exterior surface of the building-that-banks is an interface to the software that operates the abstract machine of capital. The interface there presents and represents both those operations and that abstraction as an indexical forma-tion of word/devices through which one's intentions for the capital are both expressed and materialised as legally binding actions. Finally, the decentralisation of the bank/banking interface from a bounded site to a mobile or ambient disposition of accounting subjects is enabled by web-based banking interfaces, Pocket Quicken, etc. In each case the relatively stable informational programme of "the bank" is made physical by different systems of software, and different interoperations of interfaces in and on built space.

Figure 3: Gallery = Monitor. Electronic Orphanage, Chinatown, Los Angeles. Miltos Manetas's metaphysical white box of the gallery is replaced by the hyper- and transphysical black cube of the monitor. Gallery-goers approach a huge glass void and peer through at the larger than life media displayed within/upon. The mise-en-abyme of this frame-within-a-frame digital strategy dissolves the condition of location into that of the generalised encounter with a generalised interface. Work screened above is Falling Strawberries by Mike Calvert.

Such mutation of architectural programme into software programme, in no way reduces or dematerialises the physicality of social power over the processes at hand. Even in/on the network, authority substantiates itself spatially. Software organises the world in its own image, but does so as specific, located expression of particular architectural contexts (and vice versa). Condensed into architectural programme is a scripted argument about the character of embodied and objectified habitation to play out there. A passage way encodes movement, a wall enforces discretion, and a shelf promotes display. In the location and determination of software as environmental element, such figures of disposition (movement, discretion, display) are transcoded into apparatuses of software (interface, application, or operation). The anticipation of embodiment contained within an architectural programmematic argument, is displaced to the use-case model of the software programme. This translation is not one of immediate virtualisation, of conceiving virtual passageways, walls and shelves, but of rematerialising the pragmatic functional properties of the physical through the affordances of digital technologies. Software is now asked to do what was asked of architecture.

7. Software: Subjectivity, Space

Software into subjectivity. The doubled-role of software as both a descriptive and inscriptive regime allows it to condition the productions of subjectivity in its image from both directions, figuring encounters accordingly from the very small to very large. In its descriptive mode, software is a medium though which animate space expresses itself, visualises itself. Here software indexes organisational forces diagrammatically. It senses, measures and catalogues these as invisible infrastructures and also as they present themselves upon an interactive surface or into a volumetric field. As an inscriptive technology, software is able to act upon and within such fields and to (re)construct them in its own image, to determine their operation according to directed computation, and to mediate themselves *as* computation. In these inscriptions, software is a *physical discourse* through which subjectivity and space are derived. In this derivation, in the intentional encounter with the interface, subjectivity is produced in the condensation of the "subject" into the "user." This "hypercognitive" subject position interacts with software in and against the information architect's grossly instrumental grammars of the use-case. According to this design-interpretive convention, the conditions of human-machine and human-human interaction through software are produced in the reduction and expansions of significant conventions ("trash can," "contact us," "home page," etc.) into *doxic* instruments. Here, at times, technology becomes a kind of short-hand-for-thought. Just as architectural programme configures embodiment, virtualisations of particular embodied interactions ("empty trash," "save file," "go home") are contained in these interface reductions and expansions. This *cognitivist* user-subject decorporealises interaction into a labour of typing fingers, mouse-clicking hands, and desk-prone bodies, bent into the eventual agony of inertia. This is not at all to say the body disappears, but it is redeployed and reemployed according to the performative requirements of specific interface interaction requirements.

Figure 4: (a) The UnDo stress pill. Here the physiological state of "stress" is redefined as a function of software-derived discourses, a transposition of interface-encoded subject position of the 'user' into a general, biological condition of embodiment, temporality and the layering of action into place; (b) HML (Human-Markup Language), a XML-variant that purports to index the range of "socio-cultural behaviour" into a manageable scripting system so that such notoriously subjective communication-events such as tone of voice, eyebrow raising or eye contact can be noted, coded and transmitted along with a data-stream and decoded as additional, "humanising" information. Here the premise of software as a descriptive regime is extended and universalised as almost paradigmatic (if also parodic) necessity.

As it occupies the position of both language and technology, as it both describes and inscribes action, software, the form, is a Foucauldian *regime of the body*, a material construct through which the body is produced as a speaking, legible social form. Software, as the operant lifeworld technology in the network society, structures in its image the construction of individual identity. Software becomes not only a variable in the differential display of *habitus*; it becomes a grammar for the generation of *doxa*, of the conditions of the game itself. The body is produced and reproduced in the image of software, and thereby too in the structure of social subjectivity (see figures 4) these operations are considered in more detail below in relation to the "spectacle of production" and the "dramaturgy of infrastructure."

Software to space. Software produces space both by providing a medium with which to previsualise and model eventual built instantiations (software as an architectural design language) and also by instrumentalising the organisation of plan, movement, display, and habitation according to its calculations (software as a spatial organisational technology). Of these, far more critical attention has been paid to former than to the later. However, the more significant impact on the broader cultures of space may come from these "non-architectural" softwares than from the high-end polydimensional design systems receiving more critical attention. For both, as device of formation and as a technology of organisation, software focuses several challenges to the cultures of presentation, representation, and agency.

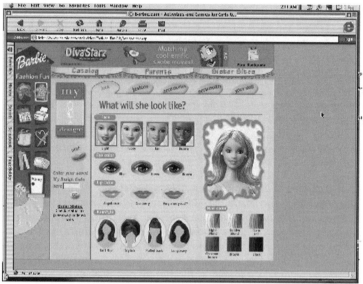

Figure 5: Make Your Own Barbie web page. Self-As-Database. As ever, Barbie stands for the idealised generic feminine subject, and here users choose from a menu of characteristics, together adding up to a complete self-subject. Their combination of choices, however peculiar, is then rendered as a doll and mailed to them for their custom play and projection. Here Barbie (and the projected self-identification of the person playing with her) is derived as database operation of a compossible field of attributes and specific values.

Architectural process (from ideation, to model, to schematic and section, to plan, to construction documentation, etc) is always already a sequential system of translation and formal transposition, one over which a designer's control and influence is limited by the conventions and constructions of these mediations. As such the interjection of software into this translation cycle, particularly at the modelling stage, inevitably modulates the conditions of spatial investigation and expression, and does so in a manner equally determining of those conditions as the pen or clay.

Early CAD was resolutely simulationist. The criterion of success was the extent to which digital models resembled in every detail, comprehended architectural form. The verisimilitude criterion directed the question as to whether software, as a modelling regime, was as good as, as complete as, as significant as the known traditional methods of form-conception from which architecture is and has been derived. As early versions of modelling-ware where used in real design and construction processes, it became clear, to the dismay of some, that software was not an innocent or transparent medium, and it contributed to if not determined the kinds of spatial investigation and expression possible to undertake with them. Many buildings from this period (late 1980's-early 1990's) are readable as having been designed not only by a certain architect, but also with a certain software! In some cases, the discursive technology of the copy/paste operation is directly legible in the semiotic seriality of the resulting structure.

Figure 6: (a) Michael Graves. The Institute for Theoretical Physics at University of California, Santa Barbara (1990). The assembly of colourful geometric primitives onto broad sequence of cartoonish flat fields: cut, copy, paste, paste, paste, paste; (b) The creative autonomy of the digital line: Hernan Diaz-Alonso's "Emotional Rescue" in SCI_Arc's Main Gallery, Summer 2002. Maya was originally a character-animation software and now the standard for post-Euclidean architectural form-exploration. In conceiving "the monster" Diaz-Alonso animates an iterative spline system within Maya to produce an enveloping complex of otherwise undrawable perspectival line-densities. Two collisions are at work: that of Maya on the virtual physics of architectural form, and of architectural investigation on the software itself. At issue is both the materialisation of autonomous digital experimentation, but also the impact of architectural investigation on the software itself.

Software's "contribution" quickly became the ends as well as the means, and the "autonomy," if not precisely the agency of software, has driven matters ever since. If early explorations were reactionary in their hopes, contemporary investigations are concerned with the direct autonomy of digital form as a domain of spatial investigation. The pursuit is of radically new forms, otherwise unimaginable, undrawable by traditional architectural media. The gravity of investigation into the resulting blobs has produced a uniquely *digital architecture*, one derived by the design of a performative mathematics of structure, iteration, repetition and involution. Framing current debate are questions and solutions as to how this "autonomy" can be devirutalised from the realm of software into the atomic worlds of built space. Furthermore, the experimental deployment of more and more non-architectural software for directly architectural means (for example Frank Gehry's use of CATIA, originally *aerospace* design software) further complicates the professional specificity of architecture and the architect, restaging both, redividing the labour of design, according to now-multidisciplinary tool sets. However I would argue that more powerful mode of software-generated space is not formal, but *logistical*. "Flow" is Manuel Castells's (and others') signal term for the operation of software, capital and architectonic space into an integrated temporal stage for mobile bodies and their mobile epistemic circuits. Here the ebb and undulation of bodies and artefacts moving through urban and networked spaces are conceived in parallel with the topographic condensations and incorporations of dataflow. Here, biographical and infomatic networks interoperate in a constantly reconfiguring complex of variable solidity and conditional duration. The movement of solid forms (think of traffic flow software, import/export production algorithms, etc.) is positioned as a central architectural function and condition, one which expresses itself as both the solidity of building systems that mediate the flow of bodies and things, and the software that animates and makes itself manifest in these human and nonhuman operations.

Figure 7: The Aesthetics of Logistics: Storage is Display. The structured space of the Big Box is a representation of a spreadsheet. It is space in the image of the database.

Not just a technology for the previsualisation of space, software is an underlying network that locates a site as an *instance of site* within the larger abstract space of global capital. A site materialises as a way station for objects organised by their trajectories of displacement, from production to consumption. In this the "Big Box," retail space is architecture emblematic of the space of flows. Here the database drives the spatio-economic form, drives the architectural form, drives the instrumental display of and encounter with a world of things. This consumption interface is designed not according to the ocular mystification of commodity forms that occupied Walter Benjamin, but as an *aesthetics of logistics*. Within the scheme of the developer, retail space, materialises the calculation of risk as strategic architectural deployment, an interface between commodities and their localised destinies as integers of shopping and buying equations. The Big Box is an expression of the calculations of exchange, a space that is excruciatingly over determined by the softwares of flow, risk, cost, benefit, circulation, etc. that govern this dissimulation of retail: *architecture as spreadsheet*. The shelf itself is a two-way orifice from the distributed markets of production to this site/habitat and to its terminal encounter with the shopper who in turns calculates its differential values for him/her within her own life, now modelled as individuated, digitally-modelled corporation. By action or inaction, buying or not buying, she encodes a commanding signal back through the space of flows to recalculate future production in accordance with the mercurial vagaries of end-user preferences. The new mall is not as much a posturban centre, as a "machine that bears things."

Academic architecture has some trouble making this transition from the commodity as fetish to the commodity as logistical meme. Some, however, have made the questioning of this transition, or at least the eclipse of the sublime, opaque commodity, into a central matter of design. In his catalogue essay on the work of Elizabeth Diller and Ricardo Scofidio, Aaron Betsky writes, "these hybrid architects/artists create work that makes visible the technologies of desire and the surveillance of objects and people. In doing so, they construct an alternative to a culture of display in which the continual presentation of goods appears to be the central task of our social and economic system. In short, these artists display *display*."[15]

The everyday Big Box, ironically, synthesises a similar operation toward radically different ends. There display is boiled down to the perfunctory purpose of storage. For database-driven space and the

---

[15] Aaron Betsky, "Display Engineers," in Betsky et al., *Scanning: The Aberrant Architectures of Diller + Scofidio* (New York: Whitney Museum of American Art, 2003) 23-36.

aesthetics of logistics they inform, display is storage and storage is display. The Big Box commodity is dramatically underthemed, stacked vertically and horizontally, situated by the barest of theme (bedding, appliance, media, etc.), the matrix of display is more specifically deployed as a means to channel attention toward generic items that, according to the software, require higher rates of purchase. The Big Box commodity is signified by a tag that contains much of its differential attributes and values as cellular data within the meta-database that operates both the business and the store architecture itself. This is its interface from production to consumption. This is the thing as data.

8. The Spectacle of Production, the Dramaturgy of Infrastructure

The reflexive circuits mapped above can be understood as a general condition in which bodies and objects assume the conventions of the other. Within this, the aesthetics of logistics names a specific momentum of these assumptions. This is considered in some detail below. Software, like architecture, is not only a technology of space; it is a medium of collective representation. It is a figure in which and through which the tumult of material culture stages and frames itself, a discourse of cognition through which collective and individuated lives index, calculate and display their desires of communication, a syntax of production mapping its own truths into the verifications of presence and absence. Software, perhaps unlike "new media," doesn't need humans to accomplish these. Software is happy to talk to other software, database to database. We not uninvited to join the conversation provided we speak the lingo, but we are not natives. Accordingly, attention regarding the directionality of transcoding moves from software simulating collective representation (GUI) to collective representation simulating software (Friendster, Quicken, the botched Florida election ballot, etc.) But any technology of collective representation is only every partial in its scope and so it is not exactly that "the world becomes interface." Instead, software, incompletely, *refictionalises infrastructure* in its own image. The classical model of Modernity tells us that superstructure makes structure opaque, that the cultures of capital obfuscate technologies of production. To remedy this misdirection we are to employ tactics of cognitive mapping to make clear what is hidden and thereby defeat the strategies of power. But now the politics of revelation and clarification are *keen branding*.

The reflexive comprehension of the procedures, mechanisms and choreographies of Modern production is not enlightenment, it is a content play; it is Reality TV as an epistemology of the Thing.

Consider two moments in fashion, that high artificialisation of the body. Consider Issey Miyake, instead of working away in his secret castle, installing his means of creative production in the gallery space, and their tailoring clothes on the spot from vast palettes of raw fabric. Here is the process, disembedded from the fiction of Modernity, embedded as a transparent fiction of calculation. Consider the little LCD's that hang among the clothes at Rem Koolhaas's SoHo Prada store. On them cinematic biographies (genealogies) of the garment's production are screened, literally broadcast onto each, not as a guarantee of its quality but as a visual literature of its specificity in the space of flows and semiotic calculation. As the theory of reflexive modernisation would suggest, this disembedding and re-embedding of the technologies of Modernity into an aesthetics of order operates as a metafiction of the social object and the social as object. Here production itself, the infrastructure of industrial and post-industrial fabrication is itself the content of its own post-spectacular content play.

One needn't pursue the heights of avant-garde fashion to discover that the software-driven rationalised administration of space, while perhaps overwhelmed by the demands of function and utility, also produces another: *the spectacle of transparent production.* "Display," as Betsky describes it in his essay on Diller + Scofidio, is still a cynical version of Benjamian aura, a sublime symptom-space of inanimate exhibitionism. But the Big Box retail typology-of-the-Thing enrolls a different tension. There the store's strategy of display is *storage*, and its strategy of storage is *display*. Ask the clerk at your supermarket if he has any more sardines "in the back" and he'll look at you like you're nuts. Paul Virilio maps the contemporary careers of globalisation and computation as parallel trajectories around a double-helixed formation, and it is not just Big Box Space that is overinfused with this *aesthetics of logistics*. In fact for all the architectonic forms of reflexive modernity, from airports to hotels, to automobiles, to housing to the romantic exchange of credit reports, storage is display. In all of these the fundamental communicative logic is *stage-managing the lifecycle of production*. This is one way that the invisible hand of culture finds to produce architecture in the image of the software through which it materialises and iterates itself.

And so here the blending of architectural programme and software programme has not everything to do with people and quite a lot to do with objects (and after Latour, "quasi-objects"). The spatial programme of this software space, here understood as the deliberate coordination of utility with circulation, the primacy of spatial consumption over spatial production, is a matter of designing the displacement and placement of things. As such the "architecture" of the Big Box, an anonymous Supermodern shed, is not really the most interesting spatial story at hand. Of greater interest (for architects, for media designers, for capitalists, for consumers) is the narrative organisation, display/storage, of the gravities of the inanimate that comprise and compose this labyrinth: eye level, brand continuity, aisle end placement, just in time inventory kit of parts, alphabetical; a database-driven sculpture of cargo.

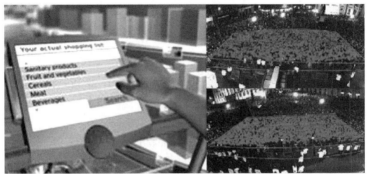

Figure 8: (a) FutureStore folds the rhetorics of supply-chain management into the seduction of consumption: self-management through objects as self-construction; (b) SpaceSyntax allows for the comprehensive visualisation and management of collective habitation of space as a dynamic field of quasi-intentional, quasi-atomic subject machines.

The (computational) spectacle of production informs and is informed by the interface-driven rationalisation of *consumption*. The microeconomic subjectivities staged by the environments of physical software perform and coordinate their purchasing decisions amongst fields of evocative commodities that now directly signify their own categorical values. At the METRO Group's FutureStore in (Germany) apples are not just red and delicious, they literally broadcast their differential value to the shopper as he navigates the supermarket space, and appear to him as a choosable option on an interface screen narrating this operation of goods acquisition.[16] The infrastructure of commodity organisation within the supermarket space, conventionally understood as an invisible backstage machine, here becomes the literal interface through which the postauratic display of goods is encountered and activated as a moment of economic seduction. The database behind the shelves is promoted as the very face of value.

---

[16] See http://www.autoidcentre.org

In this store, certainly fancier than your local supermarket, but not nearly by as much as a margin as its sponsors would have us believe, RFID tags (Radio Frequency Identification Device) individuate and identify each object from the others, specify its categorical purpose, verify its flow of origin, and communicate its costs to sellers and buyers. These tags are more articulate UPC bar codes, but which instead of communicating on behalf of a product only once it is handled and submitted to the direct gaze of a laser at point of purchase, the RFID's involve the product in a logistical narrative from point of origin to site of display and sale to point of use, blending the stages of production and consumption into a continuous, database-driven, interface-operated computational field. The physical architecture of the store (should, we assume) anticipates this rearrangement of circulatory programme in the image of software programme, and repositions itself as theatre not only of commodity display but also of environmental computation in which the shoppers and things perform the work of seduction, valuation, calculation in mutual concert.

Designing spatial circulation in anticipation of their optimal choreography is surely a problem to which architects have much to say, and according to the aesthetics of logistics, circulation is equally interested in the movement of people in inanimate space as it is in the movement of inanimate things to people. The SpaceSyntax programme at the Bartlett School of Architecture in London seeks to "understand the effects of movement on the functional performance (of built space) – in terms of passing trade, property value and natural surveillance – (thereby) increasing value and reducing risk in the development process."[17] The programme's literature continues, "we use software to model movement at all scales, from entire city networks to public space layouts and individual room arrangements." The intelligence generated by this programme is used both to "diagnose" pathologies of existing structures according to how human flows make use of them, and to in turn propose architectural options in better performative conversation with the topological contours of crowds and their differentially motivated behaviours. Here the ebb and flow of the body become circulation chain unit, stages the subject of space in extensible terms with the software that populates store shelves with smart commodities. This programme generalises the logistics of flow to a condition of all habitats and indeed all space, one which differentiates between humans and non-humans only accord-

---

[17] See http://www.scs-mag.com/reader/1998_08/vio0898.htm

ing to their fluid capacities to switch between the positions of actor and actant (in Latour's terms) in any specific context. The technology (really a series of technologies) behind much of the emerging design of supply chain object flows is the RFID. Among these MIT's EPC (Electronic Product Code) represents to many analysts the most promising direction for future development.[18] Within the EPC system, any object would be fitted with a (very very small) identification tag that when in the general proximity of a reader would broadcast specific information describing the object to a global network based on existing standards that would form the backbone of a "free, open internet of things." In proximity to a reader (at a loading dock or on a store shelf, for example) the tags on each object "wake up" and announce their identities to the network. These identities are then routed to a computer running software called Savant, which in turn sends these EPC's to an Object Name Service (ONS) running somewhere else on the network. The ONS matches each EPC to a stored address identifying each unique object. This information can be updated and augmented by Savant systems around the world. A second server uses PML (Physical Markup Language) to store comprehensive data about that product (what it is, who made it, where it came from, what colour is it, etc.). Each movement of an object is recorded as a call to the ONS and PML servers and the entire lifespan of a single thing is thereby both describable and designable.

Just as SpaceSyntax may be seen as an inversion of the FutureStore along the human/object axis, RFID technologies are by no means limited to the inscription of things that now speak their own agencies in the network. It is an equally useful system for the objectification of people and their activities. *Supply Chain Services*, an industry trade magazine, reported recently on the use of (RFID systems) to administrate the migrant farm labour and labourers.[19] The work of individual labourers is policed with great precision and the difference in pay scales for certain activities like washing up as opposed to sorting product, is monitored by this system literally inscribed on the bodies of the workers. This system is apparently not without difficulties, and the immediate content of its aesthetics of logistics surely a matter of interpretation. Mike Wiegert, account manager for Doane Agricultural Services Company, has encountered worker anxieties sparked by new technology. "With many migrant workers, especially [those] from South America, Mexico,

18   See http://www.syscan.com/w3/rfid_lm_e.html
19   See Levin and Weibel, *cntrl [space]: Rhetorics of Surveillance from Bentham to Big Brother* (Karlsruhe: ZKM / Cambridge, Mass.: MIT Press, 2002).

and Russia, having something that beeps at them scares them. If they see a red beam, they really react. Some think you're stealing their spirit or soul. It takes a little while working with them for them to believe you're not hurting them." The interpretation of the interpretation, as Mr. Wiegert's comment demonstrates, is equally problematic.

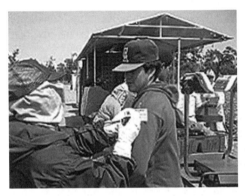

Figure 9: A farm worker being scanned by a rubber-glove wearing information technician who is able to determine exactly how much labour has been extracted from this actant.

The conversion of bodies into data-objects by RFID systems is by no means limited to human bodies, and perhaps the most informative examples to consider are in agribusiness and the livestock industries. Syscan markets a system called MeatTrak, which uses subdermal RFID's to identify parts of animal bodies after they have been dismembered in a meat packing facility and while they move from processing machines to delivery trucks.[20] Each piece of the body/ individual product piece is identifiable along the process of transforming the carcass into the commodity. According to Syscan's literature, recent occurrences of livestock diseases highlight the need for such a tracing system "throughout the entire distribution system for all products designated for human consumption." Here the fluid convertibility of bodies and objects within the active network is given a somewhat gruesome edge.

9. Conclusion

What becomes clear is that software's dual quality as a language and a technology allows it to operate on several registers simultaneously in the production and consumption of material culture, and it is precisely this convertibility that characterises its regime. The

[20] See Massumi, "Strange Horizons," in *Parables for the Virtual: Movement, Affect, Sensation* (Chapel Hill: Duke University Press, 2002).

triangular reflexivities of subjectivity, software and space are mutually productive, and one can enter this triangle at any point and continue around its points in either direction. (1) Social needs and habits determine syntactical conventions of software and user-interfaces, which provide precondition to the functional operations realised in architectural programme, form and surface (which in turn train the continuously variable forms of social needs and habits). (2) And/or software and user-interface conventions constitute a system language of emergent modernities through which irregular but mutually dependent subjects act, express and engage their different horizons of opportunity, and through which the durable forms of architecture are appropriated and augmented according to the distributed flows of those very emergences (which in turn generates the conditions of convention informing the software). (3) And/or the enveloping and extensional contours of the built environment situate the habitual and improvisational performances of social subjectivity, and the point of physical interface between networked information and networked actors/actants (which themselves reform those contours in their own images).

In this software-driven network of actors and actants, an aesthetics of logistics emerges as a determinant and derivation of reflexive modernity, one for which the representation of production and the production of representation flip roles in a kind of permanent sinusoidal oscillation producing an cultural/ infrastructural strobing pattern in which and across which everyday life engages. The discursive technology of simulation is key to this. Here, as the same software is used to premodel and previsualise planned scenarios as is used to remotely administer the organisation in question, the circuits between presentation and representation, production and consumption, twist into ever smaller braids. Simulating a war and running a war (Autometric's BattleScape war planning/ execution visualisation software, Kees Van Der Heijden's scenario planning for Shell Oil), planning your day and running your day (Quicken, Outlook Friendster), virtualising a city (MVRDV's *DATATOWN* or ElectronicArts's game, *SimCity*) and governing a city: the simulation of reflexive modernity *is* reflexive modernity.

If so, the "new medium" on which to focus our attention is *the city* (but we already knew this, didn't we?) Traditional New Media (to coin a phrase) like the internet, phone networks, and video games, have consumed themselves into the frame of the "glowing glass rectangle" and have driven their intellectual and financial investments toward the production of proprietary artistic and informational "content." But infrastructure (which means both the existing city and a new kind of city) is where this fascinated attention on "content" will move to "form." Without reifying this distinction, consider that what Thomas Y. Levin and Peter Wiebel call *CNTRL Space* is all about *visualisation*. In this remarkable exhibition at ZKM, emergent media and their power over in phenomenal and corporeal space are located in a Modern genealogy of surveillance, of perception as a mode of governance. In this, one's habitual and navigational locations in this space of metaperception are staged according to core variables of transparency and opacity, to what is seen and signified. Clearly this drama between what is *screened* (shown) and *screened* (hidden) is central to our visual modernities; but it itself, as the system that we *can* see, hides other formations and machinations, behind and beneath its visible surface (and outside the glowing rectangle).

Back to the body, this is the tension between perception and *proprioception*. Brian Massumi argues persuasively in his consideration of the embody-ability of radical digital-organic architectural forms ("Strange Horizons"), that *topology* is not an abstraction or idealisation of spatial experience, but instead a primary horizon through which the contours of habitat are encountered and expressed. Close your eyes. Walk around your room. The space you navigate—partition there, surface here—is topological. It is not composed of perceptive, semiotic cues, but topologic form. Massumi suggests that proprioception, the body's ability to measure and navigate space, not by visual or auditory perception of immediate information, but according to its own internal rhythms of relative displacement, foot pacing away from foot, arms swinging in front and back, is a primary corporeal investment in embodied space. I suggest that for the collisions between software, subjectivity and architecture, the movement from the screen to the city is also a kind of proprioceptive journey. The network *topos*, its visceral incursions into habitat and the claims these make on our positions and selves, is a constitution suggesting a revision to Latour's "parliament of things," one in which the speaking thing, the things that speak through us and on our behalf, and in which we inscribe the fluid architectures of polycollectivity, request from us a generous aesthetics, not of control but of allowing *home* to follow us into the world and onto any surface.

George Legrady's *Pocketful of Memories* for the Pompidou Centre understands this.[21] Pull something out of your pocket. What is in your pockets, how did it get there? Who made it, what improbable global journey did this mundane Thing make on its way to you, how have you enrolled it in your personal dramas and habits? How

---

[21] George Legrady, *Pocketful of Memories*, ommissioned by the Centre Pompidou, Paris, 10 April to 3 September, 2001. See http://www.pocketsfullofmemories.com

has the network of displacement that brought it to you, and your own intentions for it conspired to put this Thing, however unlikely, in your pocket. Turn it inside out, empty the pocket and let us see. Legrady asks visitors to empty their pockets and enter the summary contents into a machine that is also a database. The database catalogues the total inversion of pockets that encounter it and presents an ever-growing figure of these fortuitous donations. But what is catalogued is not just a visual record of itinerant debris, it is the *depth* by which a site, any site though in this case a museum in Paris, is informed, configured, activated by the cumulative topologies of the human and non-human biographies that find themselves there. For Legrady's work, the visualisation of these accumulations points toward a kind of *parliamentary* communication (and a plural proprioception) between things, people and trajectories which are now able not only to see each other, but more importantly to account for each other. This is, as ever, a first condition of the *play* that turns culture into design.

Contributors

Louis Armand is Director of the Intercultural Studies programmeme in the Faculty of Philosophy, Charles University, Prague. His books include *Event States: Discourse, Time, Mediality* (2007); *Literate Technologies: Language, Cogntition, Technicity* (2006); and *Technē: James Joyce, Hypertext and Technology* (2003). He is also the editor of *Contemporary Poetics* (2007), *Mind Factory* (2005) and (with Arthur Bradley) *Technicity* (2006). Currently he is completing a book entitled *Entropology: Re-evolution in the Vortext*.

Roy Ascott is President of the Planetary Collegium and Professor of Technoetic Art at the University of Plymouth. He is also a visiting professor in Design|Media Arts at the University of California Los Angeles and advisor to the art|sci centre. His publications include *Engineering Nature* (2006), *Telematic Embrace: Visionary Theories of Art Technology and Consciousness* (2003), *Art Technology Consciousness* (2000) and *Reframing Consciousness* (1999). He is the founding editor of *Technoetic Arts: a journal of speculative research* and serves on the editorial boards of *Leonardo*, *LEA* and *Digital Creativity*.

Arthur Bradley is Senior Lecturer in Contemporary Literary Studies at Lancaster University. He has published widely on continental philosophy and is the author of *Negative Theology and Modern French Philosophy* (2004) and *Derrida's Of Grammatology: An Edinburgh Philosophical Guide* (2008), and co-editor (with Louis Armand) of a collection of essays, *Technicity* (2006). He is currently working on a book entitled *The Theory of Technology*.

Benjamin H. Bratton is a theorist and design strategist based in Los Angeles. He is Director of the Advanced Strategies Group at Yahoo! He teaches design and theory at SCI_Arc and co-directs the Brand Lab at UCLA Design|Media Arts. His research interests include media architecture, brand theory, biomedia, software studies and the spatial rhetorics of exceptional violence. His introduction to the new edition of Paul Virilio's *Speed and Politics* was recently published by Semiotext(e)/MIT Press. He was co-chair of ambient:interface, the 54th International Aspen Design Conference.

Pavel Černovský is completing a PhD on "The Limits of Theory / Theory of Limits" in the work of Paul de Man and Jan Mukařovský at the Philosophy Faculty of Charles University, Prague. He is the coordinator of a group research grant, "Technicity: Towards a New Critical Paradigm?"

Stephen Dougherty is an associate professor in language and literature at Volda College, Norway. His essays on literature and science have appeared in *Diacritics*, *Configurations* and *Cultural Critique*.

Christina Ljungberg has worked in Cultural Programmeming with Swedish and Canadian Television and now teaches English literature at the University of Zürich, Switzerland. Her publications include *To Join, to Fit and to Make* (1999), *The Crisis of Representation* (with Winfried Nöth, 2003), and *Insistent Images* (with Elzbieta Tabakowska and Olga Fischer). She is currently working on a book entitled *Creative Dynamics: Diagrammatic Strategies in Narrative*.

Niall Lucy is a Research Fellow with the Australia Research Institute at Curtin University. His books include *A Derrida Dictionary*; *Beyond Semiotics: Text, Culture and Technology*; and (with Steve Mickler) *The War on Democracy: Conservative Opinion in the Australian Press*.

Laurent Milesi teaches in the Centre for Critical and Cultural Theory at Cardiff University and is a member of the Joyce ITEM-CNRS Research Group in Paris. He is the editor of *James Joyce and the Difference of Language* and translator of Jacques Derrida's *H.C. pour la vie, c'est à dire* (with Stefan Herbrechter) and Hélène Cixous's *Le Voisin de zéro*. Together with Eric Prenowitz, he is preparing a collection of Cixous's shorter essays on Jacques Derrida. He is also completing a monograph on the problematic of place in Derrida, entitled *Post-Effects: Literature, Theory and the Future Perfect*.